*William Fox, Sol M. Wurtzel and
the Early Fox Film Corporation*

William Fox, Sol M. Wurtzel and the Early Fox Film Corporation

Letters, 1917–1923

Edited by

LILLIAN WURTZEL SEMENOV
and
CARLA WINTER

FOREWORD BY SCOTT EYMAN

McFarland & Company, Inc., Publishers
Jefferson, North Carolina, and London

Frontispiece: Sol M. Wurtzel (courtesy Paul Wurtzel).

To my grandfather, Sam Wurtzel
and
to Lillian Wurtzel Semenov

Library of Congress Cataloguing-in-Publication Data

Fox, William, 1879–
    William Fox, Sol M. Wurtzel and the early Fox Film Corpora-
tion: letters, 1917–1923 / edited by Lillian Wurtzel Semenov and
Carla Winter.
        p.   cm.
    Includes index.
    ISBN 0-7864-0857-X (softcover : 50# alkaline paper) ∞
    1. Fox, William, 1879– — Correspondence.   2. Wurtzel, Sol
M., 1890–1958 — Correspondence.   3. Fox Film Corporation.
I. Title.   II. Wurtzel, Sol M.   III. Semenov, Lillian Wurtzel,
1913–1997.   IV. Winter, Carla, 1951–   .
PN1998.3.F69A4   2001
384'.8'092 B 21— dc21   00-18056

British Library Cataloguing data are available

Cover image ©2001 PhotoSpin.

Manufactured in the United States of America

McFarland & Company, Inc., Publishers
    Box 611, Jefferson, North Carolina 28640
    www.mcfarlandpub.com

Contents

Acknowledgments

Receiving this manuscript from Lillian Wurtzel Semenov was like being handed a treasure trove of family jewels—jewels that I knew should be on display. To publish these letters would be to reveal the long unacknowledged role of the Wurtzel family in Hollywood's early history. Thus publication became my mission — and one of the most difficult challenges I had ever undertaken. I am grateful to everyone who has had a role in meeting that challenge:

Sol Wurtzel — may he finally be recognized for his role in Hollywood history.

Sam Wurtzel — my grandfather and the youngest brother of Sol. Sam got Sol his first job with the Fox Corporation. Sam worked quietly, without ego or pretense, as a unit head for 20th Century–Fox until retirement, always allowing Sol the prestige and glamour.

Lillian Wurtzel Semenov — daughter of Sol, for her years of dedication in compiling this manuscript and for empowering me to pursue its rightful place in history.

Paul Wurtzel — son of Sol, for his wise counsel, direction and support.

Debora Semenov Rosen — granddaughter of Sol, for her reasonableness after the death of her mother, Lillian, in resolving and allowing my continuance on the project.

Paula Wurtzel-Parness, for supporting Lillian in daily work, encouraging her to complete the book back in the '70s, and being her best friend.

Susan Fox-Rosellini — for representing the Fox family with intelligence and wisdom.

Ellen Gameral — of the Fox Feature Story Files. As a lifetime family friend as well as a lifetime Fox employee, Ellen was instrumental in opening the path that led to publication.

Alison Pinsler — of the Fox Library. She was the conduit through which the publishing connection was made.

Alan Adler — Fox archivist, supporter of truth, and resource.

Scott Eyman — Hollywood historical authority and author, who truly believed in the value of the book and its significance in Hollywood history.

M.J. Bogatin — legal counsel, board member, California Lawyers for the Arts.
— Carla Winter

Foreword

by Scott Eyman

In Richard de Mille's delightful *My Secret Mother: Lorna Moon*, he reports that after his biological father, William de Mille, died in 1955, inquiries were made about his diaries. He was informed that de Mille's wife had thrown the diaries out. The reason: "There was nothing in them but facts."

Welcome to the difficult world of film history, whose primary drawback has always been an over-reliance on anecdotes told by professional fabulists, often speaking 50 or more years after the fact.

Historians of any degree of seriousness cannot help falling on those infrequently published books of primary, first-generation studio documentation with the avidity of people finding the spring water of truth in a desert of tall tales.

Here is one of those books.

For five years, Sol Wurtzel, production supervisor of the William Fox studio in Los Angeles, assiduously kept copies of the correspondence that passed between him and his endlessly demanding employer back east.

Here is the story of how a great studio was built — William Fox ceaselessly carping, criticizing, second-guessing, always demanding better pictures for less money; Sol Wurtzel backtracking, placating, occasionally throwing his hands up in bafflement at the impossibility of pleasing Fox, but never walking away. And always, always getting the pictures made, and finding directors like John Ford and Frank Borzage as he went along.

As a story of the rough marriage of personality, art and commerce, this book is a particularly delightful combination of *The Last Tycoon* and *84 Charing Cross Road*, but without the sentiment. His letters reveal William

1

Fox to have been a hard man, humorless and wary, sure that all and sundry were out to feather their personal nests at the expense of the Fox Film Company.

We can, of course, lament the lack of the correspondence covering the great heyday of the studios—*The Iron Horse, Sunrise, What Price Glory?, 7th Heaven*, and the Movietone sound system that, along with Vitaphone, helped obliterate one art form and create another.

But that would be like complaining about a passing insult in a will leaving you a sizable bequest. These letters, carefully preserved and shepherded towards publication by Carla Winter and by Wurtzel's children, Paul Wurtzel and the late Lillian Semenov, make a signal contribution towards a full understanding of the industrial realities of life in an era that has too often been viewed through the amber lens of legend.

— Scott Eyman

Scott Eyman is author of *Ernst Lubitsch: Laughter in Paradise* and *The Speed of Sound: Hollywood and the Talkie Revolution.*

Preface

by Carla Winter

Lillian Semenov was elegant, extremely intelligent and a stickler for details. She was a dear cousin of mine and the daughter of movie mogul Sol M. Wurtzel.

In 1995 I asked her, "Lillian, I always understood that your dad ran the Fox Film Corporation, but what does that mean?"

"It means," she answered, "that he ran the studio in Hollywood, California. He was responsible for hirings, firings, budgets, productions, every part of the studio's operations. If you are curious, then you might find this interesting." And she handed me a treasure.

Typed on the most delicate onion skin was a meticulously transcribed manuscript entitled, "My Dear Sol." It was composed of the actual business letters of Sol M. Wurtzel, who ran the West Coast operation, and William Fox, founder of the studio.

Lillian apparently found the letters while cleaning the basement of her parents' estate. She spent years compiling these letters with the intention of sharing them, so that others might enjoy this unique and authentic perspective on Hollywood's earliest history.

Sol's official title was superintendent, but the meaning of that word has certainly changed since his time. The equivalent contemporary title for Sol's job description is Chief Executive Officer or CEO. In Hollywood vernacular, studiohead.

For some reason, the current 20th Century–Fox seems uninterested in its own early history — almost denying the existence of its pre–Zanuck roots. Here, nevertheless, is proof that those roots are real. In fact, we might note that "Wurtzel" in German means "root" — and the fox, of course, is known as sly and cunning.

Introduction

by Lillian Wurtzel Semenov

When William Fox decided to send his private secretary to California in 1917, the situation at his Hollywood studio was chaotic. There were rumors of theft, graft and general mismanagement, and he wanted a superintendent who would dedicate himself heart and soul to the Fox Film Corporation. He felt that he had found such a man in Sol Wurtzel, and time proved him right.

Fox detested the long train trip to the West Coast, and for four years the two men never held a meeting but kept in constant contact by letter, telegram and an occasional emissary. Wurtzel had to account for every penny spent by the studio and justify every independent decision that he made. Fox commanded, berated, criticized and sometimes even threw in a little praise. It was always "My dear Sol" and "My dear Mr. Fox." The younger man was expected never to forget the gratitude he owed his boss, and amazingly, he never did. Read today, their correspondence is often as melodramatic and comic as any of their countless movies.

The spectacles and features turned out by the Fox organization appalled the critics but definitely appealed to the public. The moviegoers of the 1910s and 1920s loved Tom Mix, Theda Bara, the Fox Kiddies and the Sunshine comedies. The dimes and quarters that kept rolling into Fox box-offices made it possible for William Fox to build an empire worth $300 million. By 1929, he was the most powerful and threatening figure in the entire motion picture industry. He owned fifteen hundred theaters in the United States, three hundred in Great Britain, three major studios and the basic patents for sound on film.

In one of his early letters to his protégé, Fox advised him always to "play it dead safe," something he later forgot to do himself. In 1930, in spite of his desperate maneuvers, his financiers and the Great Depression together toppled him from power, and he was forced out of his own company.

Although both men grew up on the lower East Side of New York, Wurtzel, born in America in 1890, had the advantages of a high school education. Fox, born in Hungary in 1879, was brought to the United States as an infant. He left school at the age of eleven to start working full time as a cloth-sponger and later as a lining cutter. From childhood on he saved every penny he could spare and was constantly on the lookout for new business opportunities. Wurtzel at the same age was a serious-minded student trying hard to justify his family's faith in him as a scholar.

Fox found his great opportunity when he was twenty-five. He took his savings of sixteen hundred dollars and bought a nickelodeon in Brooklyn. By installing folding chairs in the apartment above and showing short (one hundred foot) films at ten cents admission, he was able to make enough profit to buy other such showrooms. From then on, one venture expanded into another. When he found that film renting was a very profitable part of the newest industry, he set up his own rental company, the Greater New York Film Rental Co. In 1914, when he couldn't buy enough independently made feature films for his needs, he started to produce his own under the banner head of the Box Office Attractions Film Rental Co. The first such film was made from a popular novel of the day, *Life's Shop Window*, and was gratifyingly successful. Fox was now launched on his triple career as theater owner, film exhibitor and motion picture producer.

He put an experienced stage director, J. Gordon Edwards, ostensibly in charge of production, and even sent Edwards to Europe to learn the latest techniques. It was against Fox's character, however, to let anyone have free rein. He was later to boast to his biographer, Upton Sinclair, that he had been familiar with every story ever produced by his company and in the early years even wrote most of the scenarios himself: "No picture ever produced by the Fox Film Company was permitted to be viewed by the general public until every title it contained had been approved and passed by me, and I don't remember a single picture ever made by the company that the titles contained therein were not corrected, edited and rewritten by me."

This kind of control was possible as long as filming was confined to the East Coast, but by 1915, Fox Film had joined the other production companies in their trend west and had established a branch studio in rented space in a section of Los Angeles known then as Edendale. Since

Fox could not be on both coasts at once, he was constantly suspicious of what was going on in California. However, he was too astute not to realize the many advantages the West Coast location held for shooting Westerns and big production scenes, and in 1916 he made the first of his very infrequent trips west to buy the Dixon Studio property on Western Avenue and Sunset Boulevard in Hollywood. He left his general representative, Abraham Carlos, in charge and returned to New York as swiftly as the Santa Fe Railroad could take him, not to return for almost ten years. Apparently this setup became increasingly unsatisfactory to Fox, and it was in October of 1917 that he sent his twenty-seven year old secretary to take over.

Wurtzel's first job after graduating from the High School of Commerce was keeping books for a wholesale grocery concern. He lost his second job, as bookkeeper for a cigar factory, during a nationwide economic slump, and he was out of work for months. His younger brother, Sam, who had been working as a clerk at the Box Office Attractions Company, decided he would rather go to agricultural school and casually suggested that Sol apply for his job. The now desperate bookkeeper put necessity ahead of pride and was willing to take a cut in prestige and salary.

Within a year he had been promoted to the post of secretary-stenographer to Charles Levin, secretary of Fox Theaters, at a salary of $15.00 per week. Then, in February of 1915, Fox reorganized his company and renamed it the Fox Film Corporation. He was dissatisfied with his current secretary and asked Levin to find him another one. Sol Wurtzel was recommended, and after a thirty day trial period the job was made permanent. Fox was delighted with him and soon promoted him to the position of private secretary. Fox commented to his brother-in-law, Jack Leo, "This young man is highly capable — has a tremendous capacity for absorbing work — is intelligent, aggressive and, surprisingly very well-read."

According to Leo, who was an executive of the company, Fox gave his new secretary plays and stories to read and asked him to furnish synopses and opinions "as to their worthiness as Fox Film productions. Wurtzel attacked these extra assignments with real enthusiasm. He studied every phase of production and his average day lasted from 9 A.M. to midnight. He was sent to Hollywood to assume the Herculean task of getting production in order at reasonable costs. There the latent ability of which he was possessed came to the fore and served him and the corporation extremely well."

Wurtzel continued to serve the company for twenty-eight years. He was devoted to William Fox and accepted his outbursts of rage and sarcasm with the humility of a dutiful son. As the years passed, he himself would become a master of the Fox style. In 1917, however, Wurtzel was an introverted, sober young New Yorker who had never traveled farther than Coney Island and the Adirondack except in his day dreams. He was apprehensive about moving his wife and four- year-old daughter, Lillian, to a totally new environment. It was finally Hettie Gray Baker, who had come from the coast to be head film editor for Fox, who successfully encouraged him to take the step. Wurtzel in turn persuaded his boyhood friend, Lewis Seiler, to give up his job teaching high school and to accompany him west as his assistant. Seiler, a bachelor, didn't need much persuasion. Tired of knocking heads together in order to maintain discipline, he was ready for the opportunities offered by an exciting new world.

Thoroughly briefed and lectured by his boss and well provisioned for the long train trip by apprehensive relatives, Wurtzel and his pal Seiler departed from New York on October 12, 1917. Five days later they checked into the celebrated Hollywood Hotel. With its vine-covered verandas, beautiful gardens and popular Thursday night dinner dances, it was the favorite hotel of the motion picture people and the vacationers from the Midwest. He wrote his wife that it was the most wonderful country in the world and begged her to come as quickly as she could.

Supplied with a shiny new Hudson and a driver, Wurtzel went to visit his new domain. The studio was less than two miles from the hotel and occupied thirteen acres of a former lemon grove. Although the equipment was of the most modern type, including two glass stages, two wooden stages and six in the open air, the workshops and laboratory were still surrounded by lemon trees. Cecil Bruen roses and honeysuckle vines climbed over the original farmhouse and the three small bungalows that were used as offices. The setting was definitely pastoral.

Western Avenue divided the property into an east and west side, and the Sunshine Comedies were filmed on the east lot. Supposedly an autonomous unit, it was currently under the supervision of Henry "Pathe" Lehrman — a disciple of Mack Sennett. The Fox two-reelers were advertised as "The Best Comedies In The World," and the urbane Lehrman had recently been hired to make the product live up to the word.

While Hank Mann, Ford Sterling, Lloyd Hamilton and other comedians cavorted on the east side of the avenue, a company of leading men and ladies went through their antics on the west lot. Jewel Carmen, June Caprice, Gladys Brockwell and George Walsh, Dustin Farnum and Jack Mulhall starred in the lesser productions that the studio turned out in endless succession. But the big Fox stars who really drew the crowds were that sultry vamp Theda Bara; the hard-riding hero of the Westerns, Tom Mix; and the handsome, curly-haired William Farnum.

Appeasing all of these temperamental beings was just one of Sol Wurtzel's many duties. He supervised every phase of production, including the comedies, from scenario to cutting room floor. He viewed every foot of the daily rushes and signed the weekly paychecks of the hundreds of employees. Even the heads of the technical departments reported directly to him. For these superhuman labors he received $100 a week — exactly one-third the salary of the man he replaced.

William Fox always recognized a bargain.

The Letters

Fox Film Corporation
130 W. 46th St.
New York City
October 22, 1917

Mr. Sol M. Wurtzel
c/o Hollywood Hotel
Hollywood, Calif.

My Dear Sol:

    In accordance with the request contained in your wire of October 18th, I am sending you herewith Resolutions authorizing you to sign checks for — The Fox Film Corporation, and, Sunshine Comedies, Inc., and canceling the authority of Mr. Carlos, to take effect October 1st.

    I am also enclosing a copy of these Resolutions for your files.

    You should receive this letter by Saturday, October 27th, and I would suggest that you immediately take this up with the Bank so that the matter can be settled before Mr. Carlos leaves Los Angeles.

Very truly yours,
(signed) William Fox

New York City
October 22nd, 1917

The Merchants National Bank,
Los Angeles, Calif.

Gentlemen:

    At a special meeting of the Board of Directors of the Fox Film Corporation, held on October 19th, 1917, the following Resolution was adopted:

"RESOLVED that Sol M. Wurtzel, be and is hereby appointed General Superintendent of the Fox Film studios at Los Angeles, California, in place of Abraham Carlos resigned, and furthermore, that the said Sol M. Wurtzel be and is hereby authorized to sign checks of the Corporation."

Very truly yours,
Fox Film Corporation
Secretary

New York City
October 23rd, 1917

Mr. Henry P. Lehrman
Sunshine Comedies, Inc.

My dear Henry:

This to advise you that Mr. Sol Wurtzel, my former secretary, who is now in Los Angeles, and who, you no doubt met by this time, is entrusted with the same powers held by Mr. Carlos up to this time.

Mr. Carlos is leaving Los Angeles on Saturday and Mr. Wurtzel will be there to perform the same functions and duties as Mr. Carlos heretofore has performed.

May I ask you to be good enough to give Sol every possible assistance and advice that you can so that he can make good at his new post?

With kindest regards, I beg to remain,

William Fox

November 2, 1917

My dear Sol:

A copy of the following telegram came from Darling* who left for Australia by the way of San Francisco:

"Tom Mix states that the employment outfit in Los Angeles is taking commissions out of the pay of your artists ten percent and lunches and he believes that the commissions are divided with one of your employees stop "that this causes dissatisfaction among the artists and that they do not work willingly — you might take this up with Wurtzel who can talk further to Mix and thrash this matter out and stop the graft."

*Far Eastern Exchange manager.

I don't know whether there is any truth in the rumors that he heard in San Francisco. However, I think you ought to investigate immediately. As a general rule, where there's smoke, there's usually fire, and there might be something in this.

As you know, I caused an investigation to be made on Mr. Rogers, who was the man who handles talent in Los Angeles, and in the middle of our investigation, he left the employment of the company. I don't know who is in charge of this work now. I think it is worthy of going into the matter very, very carefully and diplomatically.

Very truly yours,
(signed) William Fox

New York City
November 8, 1917

(PERSONAL AND STRICTLY CONFIDENTIAL)
Mr. Sol Wurtzel
Fox Film Studios
Los Angeles, Calif.

My dear Sol:

I am writing these few lines to reiterate the things I have said to you when you were at my office.

I am expecting you to operate the studios in such a manner that no information of the conducting of the studios, cost of pictures, or anything that happens in and around the studios with regard to either actors, actresses, directors, scenic departments or auditing department or any branch of it, reaches Carlos or any one else outside of the studios. So far as Carlos is concerned, he is not entitled to any information with reference to the workings of the Los Angeles Studios anymore than Sheehan is.* As you know, Sheehan has not received any information with reference to the Los Angeles Studios during Carlos' entire stay. Great care was exercised by Carlos that no information reached New York through any channel, except that he himself gave out.

I want you to be sure (and you may have a hard time doing it) to leave out any and all those at the studio in any particular position, who are inclined to write and keep Carlos informed as to the workings of the studios. This might be a hard thing for you to do, as Carlos will manage to correspond and gather whatever information he can from whatever source he can. Of course, it would not do for you to tell any one not to

*Winfield R. Sheehan, General Manager of Fox Films.

write to him and give him information. The better plan would be to eliminate every one who is now at the studio who you possible imagine would give him information of any kind, nature or description. If you are in doubt as to whether he or she would give this information, you take the benefit of the doubt and leave him or her out. Play the game dead safe. The running of the studios is in your charge, and no one has the right to know what is going on, except through you.

With kindest personal regards, I am very truly yours,

(signed) William Fox

WESTERN UNION TELEGRAM

November 11, 1917

WILLIAM FOX
NEW YORK CITY

Have Leo mail me special delivery statement showing in detail giving dates of shipments and quantities of positive and negative raw stock shipped to Los Angeles from New York from May 1, 1917 to date this list should show only actual film shipped. Important that I get this immediately.

SOL M. WURTZEL

WESTERN UNION TELEGRAM

November 13, 1917

S M WURTZEL
LOS ANGELES, CALIF.

Mailing you today by special delivery list of positive and negative shipments as per your telgraphic request

WILLIAM FOX

WESTERN UNION TELEGRAM

November 15, 1917

WILLIAM FOX
NEW YORK CITY

Please inquire immediately from Brulatour or Eastman company if they ever shipped to our Los Angeles studios or other film companies in Los Angeles perforated negative film emulsion number six four ought seven and perforated film emulsion number eight seven five eight — wire me immediately after you get information giving dates when shipped and quantities.

SOL M. WURTZEL

WESTERN UNION TELEGRAM

November 17, 1917

SOL M. WURTZEL
LOS ANGELES

Will wire you Monday regarding negative and positive emulsions.

WILLIAM FOX

While this exchange of telegrams was clicking across the country, Wurtzel was busy uncovering a big raw film heist that had been taking place at the studio. He obtained signed affidavits from the men involved in which they admitted their guilt. Then in true detective story fashion, he sent off two lengthy coded night letters. The code was a very simple one; every other word being sent in one wire and the alternate words in a second one. The two combined read as follows.

WESTERN UNION TELEGRAM (copy)

Nov. 18, 1917

WILLIAM FOX, *PERSONAL*
NEW YORK CITY

Following men are directly implicated in stealing film from our factory: Davies the bookkeeper who has been here about twelve months and has charge of all film and film records Louis Ostrow who was formerly employed at studios as film cutter from July 7, 1917 to August 4, 1917 Davies handed out film, to auto trucks which was delivered to Ostrow on the outside and stored by him in warehouse first shipment of film was sent out August 7th and other deliveries were made the last one on November 3rd Total film sent out was approximately 300,000 feet including positive and negative value ninety five hundred dollar Davies covered up the shortage by falsifying records which he gave to our auditor Davies would take cameramen's reports and as soon as a production was finished he would destroy them thus making it impossible for us to check him up previous to August We therefore do not know if any film was shipped out prior to August 7th if a cameraman reported using ten thousand feet a week Davies reported to our auditor that he used fifteen thousand feet but did not give cameraman's report to auditor keeping them himself and then destroying them we caught a man by name of Horsley who runs a commercial film printing factory in Los Angeles taking film from Ostrow's man Mullen. Mullen was formerly a cameraman for the Universal and some of the film was left in his care by Ostrow who left for Honolulu on October thirty first we have signed confession by Horsley that he purchased about sixty-one thousand feet from Mullen and Ostrow we have signed confession from Mullen that he sold sixteen thousand feet to Horsley on November sixteenth for four thousand dollars also that he collected other money for film Ostrow sold to other parties and Mullen gave part of this money to Davies. Davies is bonded for five thousand dollars and we have his signed confession that he handed out to Ostrow about three hundred thousand feet of film for which Ostrow gave him eight hundred seventy seven dollars Ostrow now on his way back from Honolulu due to arrive Frisco Wednesday will have Burns man there to pick him up Davies has wife in delicate condition this is my only reason for asking your advice Ostrow is unmarried and has previous record of going to other film companies getting acquainted with their help and thus stealing film Mullen is single if Davies is not turned over to bonding company think we can recover the following from Davies nine hundred in cash from Mullen four hundred in cash from Horsley thirty two thousand feet film he now has in his vault Ostrow has two hundred dollars in Hollywood National Bank Ostrow also has car valued eight hundred dollars do not know if he is sole owner of car if Davies turned over to bonding company can recover five thousand dollars in addition to above Burns Agency bill will be about five hundred dollars even if decide not to turn Davies over to bonding company will prosecute Ostrow, Mullen and Horsley. Do you desire recovering on bond or let Davies go free send answer by straight telegram

---

WESTERN UNION TELEGRAM

November 19, 1917

SOL WURTZEL (PERSONAL)
LOS ANGELES

Everyone whom you have proven guilty by his confession or by evidence supplied to you by Burns Delivery Agency should be prosecuted to the full extent of the law Davies should have considered his delicate wife before tried to rob our company this is positive and you are directed to act accordingly

FOX FILM CORPORATION

WESTERN UNION TELEGRAM (copy)

November 22, 1917

WILLIAM FOX
NEW YORK CITY

Everyone implicated in film stealing with exception Ostrow now in custody of police — Ostrow did not return from Honolulu — warrant out for his arrest — writing you detailed letter tonight

SOL M. WURTZEL

WESTERN UNION TELEGRAM

November 26, 1917

S.M. WURTZEL
LOS ANGELES

Sent following telegram to Horsley* in reply to his telegram to me which is quoted in my telegram to him quote acknowledge your wire November twenty fifth that read as follows double quote Arthur Horsley a nephew of mine conducting his own laboratory for trade printing at Hollywood is involved in charges by your company I appeal to you to instruct your counsel to settle out of court the publicity will do irreparable injury to my name in the film trade I will personally pay the full value of the goods in which he was involved please wire me today end double quote this matter entirely out of my hands sorry that your nephew is involved Mr. Sol Wurtzel at studios has full instructions I am writing him at length and mailing my letter today he most likely will discuss the matter with you after he has read my letter again regretting that a relation of yours should be involved in this affair end quote have written you at great length on this subject and advise you that you do not talk to anyone or negotiate with anyone until You have received my letter written today if possible by all means postpone court action until you receive my letter show this telegram to our attorneys ask them to act accordingly you will show my letter written today to them when you receive it

WILLIAM FOX

New York City
November 26, 1917

S.M. Wurtzel
Los Angeles

My dear Sol:
I received a wire this day from David Horsley as follows:

"Arthur Horsley a nephew of mine conducting his own laboratory for trade

David Horsley — established first motion picture studio in Hollywood in 1911.

printing at Hollywood is involved in charges by your company. I appeal to you to instruct your counsel to settle out of court. The publicity will do irreparable injury to my name in the film trade. I will personally pay the full value of the goods in which he was involved. Please wire me today."

I wired you the contents of the telegram, and also wired you my reply to Horsley.

Horsley, no doubt, will pretend that he is thoroughly acquainted with me, and my friend. I have heard his name mentioned, and probably have met him, but I do not remember him. In my opinion, his excuse that if his nephew is sent to jail, it would irreparably injure David Horsley's name is beyond my understanding. I would hardly want to be held responsible for the action of every man by the name of Fox. I do not see where their actions would either help or injure my name, nor do I think that the action of the nephew of Mr. David Horsely would either help or injure his name. If David Horsley was so vitally interested in his nephew, and only because he is his nephew, he probably could have kept him straight and honest. What other motive has David Horsely in the affair?

Under the laws of the State of New York, if you charge a man with being a thief, and then if you accept money from that man and withdraw your charge of theft, you lay yourself liable to indictment by our Grand Jury. This law was enacted to prevent an unscrupulous person from charging another with being a thief, for the sole purpose of blackmailing him out of money. Therefore, once the charge of theft is made, under the laws of the State of New York, you are obliged to go through with it, or you may withdraw your charge, but there must be no monetary consideration, and before withdrawing the charge, usually there is a set of papers prepared by the complainant and signed by the defendant, wherein he agrees to hold the plaintiff free and harmless, if he does withdraw the charge. In many instances, the withdrawal of the charge depends entirely upon the sanction of the District Attorney of the City of New York. If the crime was committed in the City of New York, the District Attorney must consent to the withdrawal of the charge, which he rarely does. In other words, once a man is found to be a thief, the law provides that he must receive his just punishment.

My object in writing at length on this subject and explaining the law to you, is so that you may thoroughly understand how to conduct yourself in this matter. I am not familiar with the laws of the State of California, and I am wondering whether or not Mr. David Horsley is setting a polite little trap for you and the Fox Film Corporation. Before communicating with Horsley or doing anything further in this matter, be sure you show my letter to our attorneys so that they may get the thought of my mind.

In accordance with the telegraphic communications that you have sent to me, I take if for granted that the only evidence that you have is of the thefts after August 20 1917, amounting to approximately 300,000 feet of positive. It is fair to assume that this has been going on a longtime, and it is also fair to multiply our losses by at least ten. If the amount of the theft since August is $10,000, it is fair to assume that our total loss was in the neighborhood of $100,000. If the law of the state of California permits you and the Fox Film corporation to withdraw this charge, if the defendants are willing to make good that which they have stolen, then by all means the amount of settlement should be many times the equivalent of the amount you found they stole, according to your records, since August, 1917.

Under all circumstances, move slowly in this matter, and keep me properly advised before you take final action, and do not discuss anything with a single defendant or his relation with anyone else, without having a stenographer alongside of you and another witness, in whom you have confidence, so that you may have a full record of you conversations, and be sure that during your conversations, you do not for one minute take the position that if the money will be given to you, the charge will be withdrawn. That portion of the transaction must be left to our attorneys. They will proceed in a proper legal manner, which will safeguard our being involved in any way in the above proposition.

With kindest regards, I am,

Very truly yours,
(signed) William Fox

LAW OFFICES
Oscar C. Mueller & Alfred Wright

Los Angeles
December 1, 1917

Mr. William Fox
New York City

Dear Mr. Fox:

Mr. Wurtzel called this morning and we had a conference regarding the Horsley matter. Your letter was right to the point and covered the essential features of this matter.

We must exercise considerable care in our negotiations with the District Attorney's office, because we have called into play the machinery of that office.

We have an appointment to review the entire situation with David

Horsley Monday at 11:30. We will see what kind of proposition he has to make, and then let you know whether or not we believe successful negotiations can be concluded. While we don't want to prejudge the matter, we believe that Mr. Wurtzel has sized up Horsley very well and we know in advance something of the caliber of the man we have to deal with.

The charge against Davies is set for a preliminary examination Tuesday at 10:00 o'clock, and the charge against Arthur Horsley for Friday (December 7th) at 10:00 o'clock. Our acquaintance with the District Attorney and his associates has insured a complete co-operation all along the line in this matter.

The chief investigator of the District Attorney's office has taken a special interest in the case. He is the Sherlock Holmes, so to speak, of the County, but works in fact instead of fiction.

Of course there is no doubt in our minds but what Horsley knew the film was stolen. He was getting it at about a third under the market price, and his first question to the seller would naturally be, "Where did you get this film, and upon what basis do you fix this price?" Of course it is quite probable that Horsley knew that these particular parties were in the habit of selling stolen film. Of course he will take the position that he was innocent of any wrongdoing upon the part of the seller. He has a very capable and shrewd criminal lawyer employed.

Very truly yours,
Oscar S. Mueller & Alfred Wright

WESTERN UNION TELEGRAM

December 3, 1917

MR. WILLIAM FOX
NEW YORK CITY

David Horsley interviewed our attorneys and offered to pay nineteen hundred dollars value of sixty one hundred feet of film his nephew purchased — it is problematical if we can collect much from Ostrow and Mullen — please wire immediately if we shall accept money from Horsley and drop charges against his nephew — our attorneys believe district attorney will drop charges against Horsley on this basis.

SOL M. WURTZEL

WESTERN UNION TELEGRAM

December 4, 1917

S.M. WURTZEL
LOS ANGELES

I presume your wire on A. Horsley came after you had read my letter — how do we know that only sixty one thousand feet were purchased by Horsley — this might have been going on for two years — who bought the balance that was stolen understood you to say that records show three hundred thousand feet were stolen since August first — I do not consider it good policy to take this matter up by telegraph I would rather do it by the mails — in my opinion Fox Corporation has been robbed of at least one hundred thousand dollars by film stolen and nineteen hundred dollars is hardly the sum of money that would compensate them for their loss.

WILLIAM FOX

WESTERN UNION TELEGRAM

December 8, 1917

S.M. WURTZEL
LOS ANGELES

Sending following day letter to Oscar C. Mueller quote I have your letter of December first and note what you say the defense of Horsley's nephew will be — in my opinion his defense is unsound — film is a peculiar commodity everyone in film industry knows that all film made by Eastman Kodak company can only be bought through Eastman Kodak Co or its authorized agent J E Brulatour whose place of business is in New York — I have communicated with Brulatour and he informs me that Horsley family price to everyone which for perforated negative three and one quarter cents per foot plus one quarter cent per foot war tax and for perforated positive two and seventy one hundredth cents per foot plus one quarter cents per foot tax on film shipped from Rochester — when shipped from New York there is an additional charge on sixteen cents per thousand feet for transportation — in my opinion no man who is in film business length of time Horsley is can set up a defense and substantiate it that employees of any other company can sell film to him at one third of its market price without him knowing that it is stolen end quote.

WILLIAM FOX

In spite of Fox's exhortations, Wurtzel and the Los Angeles attorneys handled the Horsley matter with discretion and the nephew was not prosecuted. Davies on the other hand pleaded guilty but was given a suspended sentence.

Concurrent with the stolen film affair were the continuing problems of actual production. Fox permitted only his biggest stars to be temperamental, and he groused about every penny spent on what he considered the whims of his directors. Locations were his pet peeves and their insistence on shooting away from the lot always aroused his wrath.

The majority of the directors under contract to Fox Films in 1917 were very young men who had gotten their early movie experience at other studios. Fox saw to it that they worked heart and soul for the company. He recognized the talented ones and many were to become the Academy award winners of later years.

Scottish-born Frank Lloyd came to Hollywood in 1912 via Canadian vaudeville. After playing "heavy" parts at Universal, he began to direct and write two-reelers. His reputation as a top director was firmly established after he directed Les Misérables, Riders of the Purple Sage *and* Tale of Two Cities *for Fox. When the Motion Picture Academy of Arts and Sciences established its annual awards in 1927, he won "Oscars" for* Mutiny on the Bounty, Cavalcade *and* Divine Lady.

Raoul Walsh, another handsome young actor-turned-director, directed Theda Bara in a version of Carmen *when he was twenty-three. Over the years he directed many of Fox's greatest box office successes:* The Honor System, What Price Glory, The Big Trail, *and* In Old Arizona— *the first sound picture to be filmed outdoors.*

There was Bertram Bracken who came directly to Fox Films from a stint in the United States Cavalry and who made his mark in 1916 as the director of that popular tear-jerker East Lynne. *The oldest of the group was forty-seven year old Edward Le Saint who quit a railroad job to go on the stage. After considerable experience in the theater he joined Carl Laemmle's IMP company and was considered one of the top directors of the period.*

Fox and Wurtzel had minor run-ins with all of these men at one time or another but the bugbears of their lives were two young brothers— Chester and Sidney Franklin— the "kid directors" from the Fine Arts and Triangle studios who liked to work as a team. Although they had directed very successful versions of Jack and the Beanstalk *and* Aladdin's Lamp *at his New York studios, Fox became disillusioned with them when they returned to Hollywood. Pages and pages of correspondence were concerned with their ineptitude, faithlessness and ingratitude towards the Fox organization. The brothers survived their ordeal at Western Ave. and eventually went separate ways as directors. Sidney was later to receive acclaim and Academy awards for* The Barretts of Wimpole Street *and* The Good Earth, *and as the producer of the World War II favorite* Mrs. Miniver.

December 22, 1917

(copy)
Los Angeles
Mr. William Fox
New York City

My dear Mr. Fox:

I wish to acknowledge receipt of your telegram of December 21st, in which you ask me to give you dates when I hope to ship the next Brockwell

(Gladys), Carmen (Jewel) and Mix pictures, so that you can arrange releasing dates. With reference to the Brockwell picture, I expect to have this picture photographed, cut, and shipped on or about January 23rd.

In regards to the Carmen picture, Chet Franklin had an unfortunate experience in that he went to Truckee, Arizona to do some snow exteriors. When he got there he found that there was no snow and his is now on his way back to the studio without having photographed a foot of film. When he returns to the studio he will arrange his story so that it can be done in and around Los Angeles. I have, therefore, been unable to communicate with him in regard to when the picture will be finished; but I can safely say that it will be shipped to you about the same time as we will ship the Mix picture — in all probability sooner, as I will get after Chet Franklin and have him make up for lost time.

With further reference to the Franklins, sometime ago you wrote me a letter that, in your opinion the Franklins were working for themselves all the time and not for the Fox Film Corporation; and I replied to this disagreeing with you. However, I now admit that I was wrong, for my experience with the Franklins the past three weeks has been that they are for themselves first, last and all-the-time. Against my judgment and advice, Chet Franklin insisted upon going to Truckee, and against my judgment and advice Sid Franklin insisted upon going one hundred miles away from the studio to do some exteriors with a large company, when he could have gotten the same thing in Los Angeles.

These two experiences with the Franklin boys has taught me a great lesson. In the future I will deal with them with an "Iron hand". Mr. Lloyd, Mr. Bracken, and Mr. LeSaint don't make a move unless they first consult me, and I mean to make the Franklin boys do likewise. It is therefore possible that in the near future they may begin writing and telegraphing to you, and consequently I thought it best to advise you of this before hand. Unless these two gentlemen are dealt with firmly, they will never be able to make pictures within the cost we require of them.

I have gone over the situation at present existing in the studio very carefully for the past two weeks, and I have come to the conclusion that the system of having four directors with three stars does not work to the best interests of the corporation. It is my opinion that we should only have one director with one star, thereby saving many thousands of dollars by not having one director laying around idle for two or three weeks; for directors feel that if the star is not ready to go to work with them, they have no incentive to get ready until the star does join them. This is a disease that usually affects directors no matter know conscientious they are. I have therefore decided, unless I hear from you to the contrary, to combine both Franklins into one company after they are finished with their present pictures, and to only have four companies working — that is, Lloyd, Bracken, LeSaint and the Franklin company. If you do not agree with me on this, please wire me.

My plans for the next picture will therefore be as follows: LeSaint will do a picture with Brockwell; Bracken will do a picture with Carmen; the Franklin company will do a picture with Mix. After these pictures are done, Bracken will do a picture with Brockwell; LeSaint will do a picture with Mix; and the Franklins will do a picture with Carmen. When both Franklin companies are combined, I will dispense with one entire company so that they will have only one assistant director, one cameraman, one assistant cameraman, one property man, etc.

The reason I want to have Miss Brockwell go back to Bracken is, that when I told her LeSaint was preparing a story she refused to go with him, insisting upon having Bracken. She finally agreed to go with LeSaint, and I told her she would go to Bracken after that. This does not mean, however, that if Bracken's pictures prove unsatisfactory I will keep him for the purpose of directing Miss Brockwell; for if they are not satisfactory, I will dispense with his services and get another director for Miss Brockwell. Miss Brockwell does not want to go with the Franklins and the Franklins don't feel like directing Miss Brockwell. However, from the picture Mr. Bracken is now doing with Miss Brockwell, I have no doubt that he will continue to remain with us, for I am sure the picture he is now working on will be fully up to the standard the organization requires.

In my talk with Miss Brockwell she mentioned to me that sometime ago Mr. Carlos told her she would do the story *Resurrection* by Tolstoy. I told her that we had already made this story three years ago, but that I would communicate with you in regard to it. I would now like your advice as to whether you would want to do this story with Miss Brockwell. There is no question about her giving a wonderful performance, for she is enthusiastic about doing it; but whether it would be good policy to do the picture again I don't know and I therefore ask your advice. If you want it to be done again, I will have the scenario prepared at once.

> Respectfully yours,
> Sol M Wurtzel

> New York City
> December 27, 1917

Mr. S.M. Wurtzel
Los Angeles

My dear Sol —

I am acknowledging your letter of Dec. 22nd, in which you give a report of the various pictures now in work and the approximate dates when you will be able to ship same.

I note the unfortunate circumstances with reference to Chet Franklin's picture. I am sorry, but I am obliged to blame you for this condition. You know from past experience, that nothing suits a director any better than to hop on a train with his company and go somewhere, no matter where it is, as long as he can get away from the studio. This is the kind of work practiced in Los Angeles and likewise in New York by the majority of our directors. We have in our employ a few directors who are conscientious and who have the executive ability of finding out before they go to a location, whether the location they are going to is really ready for them to photograph. To prevent a director who has not the mentality or business insight, because he has never had any business training and because he has always spent the money of motion picture producers in a haphazard way, from making unnecessary trips, it is our duty to first discover what he is going away for, where he expects to go, and then it is our duty to find out whether the condition the director is going for, is really to be had at that location.

There is a telephone communication between Los Angeles and Truckee, and also a telegraph communication. When I was in Los Angeles, Raoul Walsh had occasion to go to Truckee to make the *Silent Lie*, with his wife,* for which he required snow. We wired and had positive information, that that country was available for us and that we could get the things we required, and that there was snow there. This was done before Walsh thought of leaving Los Angeles. Of course, you can charge this up to experience, for this will occur any more times, unless you guard against it by using the telephone or telegraph, which is at your disposal, to the location where your troupe hopes to go, to discover whether the things are there that your director is going for.

I have written this first paragraph after only reading the first page of your letter, and I am going to leave it stand as it is, although after reading the remaining portion of your letter, I can understand just what is occurring.

You are perfectly right in saying that you will deal with the Franklins with an iron hand, and you should deal with them with an iron hand. They are working for the Fox Film Corporation under the terms of their contract, and they will be expected to carry that contract out. That contract is specific and they are obliged to conduct themselves in a manner satisfactory to the Fox Film Corporation. I would not advise losing your

Miriam Cooper — the actress.

head in this matter. You must do this in a diplomatic and sane way, and you may make it very clear to them that up to the present time, all of the films made by them for Fox Film Corporation, while they are really good films and while they are going to be a real big financial lift to the Fox Film Corporation because the films are ahead of the times, and because the exhibitors refuse to pay the price for them, which is caused by the public not being willing to patronize theaters to see kiddie pictures.

I have not examined the Franklin brothers' contract. I am under the impression that that contract provides that they are to separate if the Fox Film Corporation desires, and to work individually, and I do not know whether the Fox Film Corporation has a right to now ask them to go together. However, the contract is plain, and your reading will give you that information. If the contract provides that we can combine these two directors again, you can do so, although it is my opinion that it will be a waste of time, for each one of these men has proven that he is capable of directing by himself, and there is nothing to be gained by having them work together, thereby causing a double expense of two directors for one company. I would by far rather leave our directing force in Los Angeles with the two Franklin boys, Frank Lloyd and LeSaint and leave Bracken out.

I note what you say about Miss Brockwell, and therefore advise you that so far as I am concerned, when Miss Brockwell is through with her present picture, if she does not want to work under the terms and conditions of her contract, let her out. She means nothing to the Fox Film Corporation, in fact, in my opinion, she is a detriment to the company. Her six month option period expires May 7th, 1918. I am not interested in doing Leo Tolstoy's Resurrections, or any other story that might suit Miss Brockwell. The company has put up with pranks long enough, and it is satisfactory to me not to make another picture with her; in other words, "give her the gate" or "tie a can to her". However, before we finally let Brockwell out, it naturally will be essential that we engage someone else to take her place. I am going to scour the New York market for someone, and in the meantime, you scour the Los Angeles market, and find out who is available. Notify me by telegraph the lowest possible price any available stars can be hired for. I in return will advise our exchanges, so that they may inform uses to the popularity of the stars that you may recommend, and whether they are drawing cards at the local theaters, and whether they advise that we engage them. I likewise will do the same on any of those who I may find in and around New York.

For your information, let me advise you that I have this day engaged Miss Peggy Hyland. I did this after finding out from our exchanges of her popularity and that she would be an asset to our company, and got her services for $300.00 a week, although she was earning $1000 with the Vitagraph. I, however, require her to work here in New York to keep the directors here busy, otherwise I would have sent her on to you immediately.

Our directors here in New York are now engaged in the following way:

Buel with the Lee Children (Jane and Catherine)
Stanton with Bill Farnum
Edwards with Bara
Millarde with Caprice (June)
Harbaugh with George Walsh

I am going to have Lund handle Peggy Hyland, and I have engaged a new director to handle Miss Pearson (Virginia). We have, therefore, idle Miss Sonia Markova.* I am in doubt whether I want to make any more pictures with her. For the present, I am going to leave her idle, until I learn from the exhibitors if she is wanted. This I can only learn after her second picture is played, which is shortly to be released. If I were sure of making another picture with her I would send her on to you, but I doubt whether I want to make another picture with her, for I do not want to make any pictures with anyone whom the exhibitors do not want and which we cannot readily sell. I am reciting this to you, so that you may know I have no one here in the East that I can send on to you. So while this scouting process is in operation, you in Los Angeles and I in New York, to discover who is to take the place of Miss Brockwell, I presume you will have to make another picture with her. At the conclusion of that picture, we should be able to find someone to substitute for her, even if that be long before her contract expires. I think the company is better off to pay her salary for the balance of her contract whatever length of time that may be, depending upon how soon conditions will permit us to make the change.

I soon learned when I was in Los Angles, that the Franklin Brothers were working for the Franklin Brothers, and for the reputation they had in sight rather than the Fox Film Corporation. However, I was able, with my presence there, to get Mr. Sid Franklin to make a picture for half the cost he made any of the children pictures, and in a period of five weeks, He showed me conclusively that he can work rapidly if he wants to, and in my opinion, *Babes in the Woods* is a better picture than *The Mikado* or *Treasure Island*, both of which cost twice the money, or from what you said about *Ala Baba*, it is better than *Ala Baba*. So you see it is only a question of being able to handle these men diplomatically to get what we are justly entitled to, and this is not done by force or by "iron hand" methods but by genuine, diplomatic and manly argument, explaining circumstances and conditions, so that they may be thoroughly conversant with the fact that

Stage name of Gretchen Hartmann, wife of Alan Hale.

they cannot draw salaries without earning them, and that although they may be good directors and produce good pictures, that the pictures will not earn money for the company they are made for, unless they are made within the cost to enable our company to make a profit on them. Impress upon them in this manner that unless they do this, they will not be earning their salaries. This is a distinction I am afraid that these two boys have not got in their minds. They are evidently under the impression that so long as they have made a picture, they have accomplished all that is necessary, not considering what the company has expended on the picture, and they have not actually earned their salaries unless the company is able to sell the commodity and get in return to the commodity what they have expended for the making of the picture, including their salaries, plus a legitimate profit. If the production does not earn sufficient money to get back the original cost, then they positively have not earned their salaries, and I am sure they do not expect to draws salaries which they do not earn. If this can be brought home in a forceful and diplomatic way, I am sure you will get the ultimate results. These two men have been spoiled by Carlos who babies them, and who was under the impression that they are real hard and conscientious workers.

The little Franklin is a conversationalist, and by his conversation, was always able to convince Carlos that he was a hard and conscientious worker, instead of devoting his time to making pictures at a moderate cost, so that the company could be rewarded by a profit on his services. It ought to be a small matter for you to make clear to them that if the company employs twelve directors, and if each director works for his personal reputation, without having in mind the ultimate profit of the company, that company, no matter how much money it has at its disposal, will eventually go bankrupt, and I am sure it is not their intention to throw us into bankruptcy. If this is properly explained to them, I am sure you will have two conscientious and ambitious men. If you will make it clear that the earning power of the company is governed by the earning power of the pictures produced by its directors; that regardless of the price contained in a director's contract, if the concern earns a moderate profit on the picture during six months of the year, it always rearranges the salary of the director in accordance with the earning capacity of the pictures he produces, you will get them to see the matter in the proper light.

The Franklins have very cleverly blackjacked Carlos into an advance of salary right at the opening of *Jack and the Beanstalk** as you know, before we were able to learn what the real earning capacity of the children pictures was. You remember how anxious and urgent I was to consummate their

*An extremely successful picture with child-stars Virginia Lee Corbin and Francis Carpenter.

contract, for I felt then that the children pictures would be a sensation all over the world. I have since learned my mistake, and therefore, I am partly to blame, for I feel that my anxiety at that time has caused them to become self-conscious, and made them imagine they are an important factor in our business. During your conversation, be sure in a diplomatic way, to make it clear that it is not your object to fire them or let them out, but that you would rather pay them their yearly salary and keep them idle, so that their reputations may die, that have them be a stumbling block to your successful management of the Los Angeles Studios. Naturally, as you say, as a result of their conversations with you they are going to wire to me. That will hardly be necessary, however, if you handle this matter in a diplomatic way, for after all, your success will depend upon the good will of the men who are doing the work for you and under your management.

Lloyd (Frank) wired me today as follows: "Have just reviewed coast print of *Kingdom of Love* from laboratory end wish you could personally see it am sure you would not have such a print shown to the public under your name."

To which I replied as follow: "I am sorry that print of *Kingdom of Love* was in condition you claim I have found fault with laboratory to extent that we are shutting laboratory down for general overhauling before any more subjects of Fox Film Corporation are printed to insure against recurrence of condition you complain of sincerest regrets— wish you and those dear to you a very happy New Year."

Will you please express my deep regrets to Frank Lloyd for the poor printing on *Kingdom of Love*, for it is a little picture I love, and I am sorry it did not come out well in the printing. As I wired to Lloyd, I have finally plucked up enough courage to close down our laboratory and send the printing to outside concerns until such time as I feel our factory is thoroughly cleaned and perfected so as to insure our company of getting good printing in the future. The difficulty with our factory was that we over-crowded them, and we asked them to do more than twice what its capacity was. The factory is now being devoted exclusively to the completion of all foreign orders, at the conclusion of which, I expect to close down the plant entirely, and then start the bill all over again, so that they will be able to turn out real good work, for as you know, our prints was and still should be capable of doing good printing. Your telegram complaining about the printing of *Babes in the Woods* came in very handy, for Jack Leo was a bit obstinate and did not believe the various complaints from throughout the country and felt that someone was intentionally knocking without cause, but he took heed when you brought to our attention the printing of *Babes in the Woods*, for he knows that you are his friend and that you would not say anything that was not true.

I want to thank you for sending that telegram, and hope that in the future, you will advise me as to the condition of each subject that is shown in Los Angeles. I want your unbiased opinion. If it is good, I want you to say so; if it is no good, I welcome your criticism, for we can only improve by being criticized instead of complimented, when we are entitled to criticisms.

Very truly yours,
(signed) William Fox

New York City
January 4, 1918

Mr. Sol M. Wurtzel

My dear Sol:

I quote herewith telegram I received from Gladys Brockwell: "Mr. Fox: My mother has just had a very serious operation. It and attendant expenses put me in grave danger of rather embarrassing debt. May I again impose upon your good nature and ask an advance of five hundred dollars to be paid back weekly at the same rate as before if I may have this at once it would relieve me of a great deal of worry. Sincerely"

To which I had Pincus* reply as follows: "I have delayed answering your telegram addressed to Mr. Fox in the hopes that Mr. Fox would return so that he could give it attention. I was this day informed however he will not return until the middle of January. On his return I will be glad to bring the matter to his attention."

In view of the statements contained in my recent letter to you, wherein I stated that in the meantime if we could locate someone who can take Miss Brockwell's place, it is satisfactory to me to let her out, and not renew her contract.

I don't want to grant this loan of $500.00. You having this situation in hand should be able to judge just how long we will have to retain her services. I leave it to you to decide if you want to advance her this $500.00 and deduct it from her weekly salary. There might be a way of doing this, and take it out of her salary weekly, so that the entire amount will be paid before the expiration of her contract. Use your own judgment in this matter.

I presume the request ought to be granted, if it is for the operation of her mother; providing, however, you think we will retain her services for a sufficient length of time to deduct the full $500.00 advanced to her.

*Joseph Pincus — Fox talent scout and casting director

Very truly yours,
(signed) William Fox

Los Angeles
January 16, 1918

Mr. William Fox
New York City

My dear Mr. Fox:

We have shipped you yesterday the Positive and cut Negative of the Brockwell picture, *Jezebel's Daughter*. The cost of this picture, from the figures which now appear on our books is $17,824.00 to which will have to be added about $600.00 for bills which are to come in. This will make the completed cost approximately $18,500, including the $1000 which you paid for the story in New York and which we have charged here to the cost of the picture. I am enclosing herewith a list of suggestions, — a copy of which I have sent to Miss Baker (Jettie Gray) and which I hope will be of some help to her in titling the picture. The titling of the picture at present is decidedly off-color, and, as in Bracken's last picture, I am depending on the New York end to help me out.

In my opinion Bracken has shown considerable improvement in this picture, which entitles him to make another picture, and I have, therefore, arranged that he do the next picture with Miss Carmen. We have several stories here for Miss Carmen's next picture, but before deciding on which one, I had two of them put in scenario form, and after I read them both I will decide which one to do. Bracken will begin photographing his next picture not later than one week from today. *Jezebel's Daughter* in its present length is approximately 4200 feet, and after additional titles are put in, will come to 4300 feet, which I presume is sufficient length for the picture.

I wish to acknowledge receipt of your letter of December 28th, which I delayed answering until I could see Bracken's completed picture. After seeing this picture and deciding that it would warrant our having Bracken continue with us, I had a talk with the Franklin boys. In this talk I told them that in the future they would work together, and also explained to them how I expected them to conduct themselves in the future. I told them that in view of the fact that they seemed dissatisfied with the present management of the Los Angeles Studio that I would advise them to take up with the Fox Film Corporation the matter of releasing them from their contracts, and I told them that if I were dissatisfied with the concern I was working for and did not like the management, I would leave in a hurry. I told them that I would personally recommend, if they wanted, that the Fox

Film Corporation cancel their contracts for them and give them the opportunity of going else-where to make pictures. In other words, I called their bluff, and they fell over themselves in trying to explain that they were anxious and willing to continue to work for the Fox Film Corporation, and to conform with its methods and management. They are now like two quiet little lambs.

I had analyzed carefully everything you wrote in you letter about the Franklin boys before I made up my mind to have them work together in the future and I am sure that what I did will work out for the best interest of the company. There is not doubt in my mind after looking up the previous work of both the Franklins, the quality of their pictures, the cost of their pictures, and the length of time it took to make their pictures, that Sydney Franklin can make a picture to cost not more than $20,000. Sidney Franklin photographed his Tom Mix picture in exactly four weeks—but to do this, he worked day and night and was all in at the finish. This picture, from the figures I have before me cost $26,093. We can figure approximately another $1000 for bill which are coming in. The picture is now being cut, but from what I have seen, it shows the money that has been spent on it. In his future pictures, he will not have the big mobs that his present picture shows. This will mean a saving of money and time. However, it is my opinion, that Sydney Franklin could not photograph another such picture in less than six weeks.

In regard to Chet Franklin; it will be the greatest mistake to let him direct a picture by himself. He is like a helpless child. I will not venture to say now what his picture will cost. I am sure, however, that it will not be under $30,000. Another thing that decided me to have them work together was the fact that Chet Franklin has been put into the first-class in the draft and he may be called at any time. I did not want to be put in a position to have him start a picture and to be called to the army in the middle of it. By having them work together, I am sure that they will be able to make the pictures quicker, at a less cost, and better.

I note what you say about Miss Brockwell. I am scouring the entire Los Angeles market to find someone to take her place, but up to the present writing I have been unsuccessful in getting anyone who I think would be what we want on our program. Nearly all of the good ones are tied up with concern under longtime contracts. Those who are open and available do not amount to anything. However, I will keep on trying and as soon as I find any who are strong enough I will wire you.

Respectfully yours,
Sol M. Wurtzel

The entrance of the United States into World War I and the Spanish Influenza epidemic had a very adverse effect on the picture business in 1918. At first, audiences kept away from the theater because they felt guilty about enjoying themselves; later, because they were afraid to expose themselves to the dreaded germ.

Many companies ceased production entirely and a majority of the movie houses in the United States and Canada closed down but the Fox organization remained in good condition. The situation gave Fox an excellent excuse to pound away on his favorite theme — economy; his practical philosophy being that it was better for a few to suffer than that all should suffer. He even got Tom Mix, his biggest money-maker at the box-office, to agree to take a four week lay-off without salary.

New York City
January 21, 1918

Mr. S. M. Wurtzel
Los Angeles

My dear Sol:

You no doubt have been hearing rumors of many of the film producing companies in the east closing down temporarily and in some cases indefinitely. Many of these rumors have materialized, and during the past week almost all of the companies have shut down. In nearly all cases these producers have arranged with their help, even those who they have under contract, not to pay them during the time their companies are not working. No doubt, by the time you receive this letter many of the companies in Los Angeles will have done the same.

I am writing you this letter, not because we have any intentions at this time to reduce our forces or shut down our companies, although it is impossible at this time to tell exactly what will happen, but I believe the next two or three months will be the most critical and trying period of the picture business. I am therefore looking to our directors in the east and west to co-operate with us in every way to carry us over this present trying period so that we will not have to follow the lead of the other producers. For it is only by the co-operation of our directors, actors and technical staff that we will be able to do this.

I therefore wish that upon receipt of this letter you call in your directors and read this letter to them so that they will know the position we are in, and so that they will give you their help.

I wish that you would immediately dispose of all actors who are in stock except those who are under contract.

Go over your general payrolls with your technical staff and cut wherever possible.

There is to be no increases in salaries to anyone until further instructions from me.

Go over your company payroll and lay off all unnecessary people; by that, I mean, it may be possible for one man who now has not enough work to do the work of another man besides his own and thus save one man. I understand that both Franklins are going to work together; I therefore presume that you will lay off one entire company. With reference to the cameramen, I understand that Sid Franklin has Jenning (Devereux) and Chet Franklin has Good (F.B.). It is my wish that Jenning be retained and Good be laid off with the rest of the company until such time as we may send more companies to Los Angeles, then he is the first choice. I realize that in laying off people it will mean that men who have been with us for years will have to suffer, but this cannot be helped, it is far better that a few shall suffer than have to shut down our plant and have all suffer.

Another great saving can be made in the use of film. Negative and positive film now costs one-half a cent more, owing to the war. This means an annual increase to us in the cost of film of about $40,000 which cannot be made up, but must be charged to profit and loss. However, the directors can help us by not exposing too much film. I note that in *Cupid's Round Up*, LeSaint used about 30,000 feet of negative, whereas in *For Liberty* Bracken used only 17,000 for two negatives. Lloyd's average is about the same as Bracken's. In the Kiddie's pictures (child actors) the negative used was tremendous, however, I realize that in the Kiddie pictures this may have been necessary owing to the difficulty in directing children; however, I presume in the pictures the Franklins are now finishing the amount of negative used was near to Bracken's average, now directing grown-ups. I don't know how much film they used for I have not as yet seen their pictures. However, if the film they used runs very high, please ask them to cooperate with you. Another important thing, there is a tax of one-quarter of a cent on positive; that is on every release and for every print made there is this tax that must be paid to the government. For that reason we want our pictures in 4200 to 4500 feet, for when we make seventy prints of a subject the cost to us of the tax is tremendous. Then again, in a 4500 foot picture, where only about 4000 feet of scenes is necessary, 20,000 feet of negative ought to be enough for two negative on a picture. Suggest to your directors that only one take of each scene is necessary to be printed except on special scenes; this would be a great savings.

If your directors will help you, they will help themselves, for in my opinion this is the severest crisis of the picture business, and I want the Fox Film Corporation to come out with flying colors.

Very truly yours,
Fox Film Corporation
(signed) William Fox
President

New York City
January 23, 1918

Mr. S.M. Wurtzel
Los Angeles

My dear Sol:

I wish to acknowledge receipt of your letter of January 16th, and have carefully read its contents. I will only answer such paragraphs as require reply.

I was indeed pleased to learn that you took the position you did with the Franklin boys, and now that you have taken this position, go right through with it. They have got to learn and know that they must work to your entire satisfaction, or otherwise you are correct in saying that they must get out. I am deeply disappointed to see the cost of the Tom Mix picture and likewise the Chet Franklin picture. I am afraid they won't change these costs even if they work together, for they are working for the Franklins first, last and all the time, and the hell with the Fox Film Corporation so far as they are concerned. The remedy must come from the writing of the scenario, and the scenes that require much cost must be eliminated. Unless you do that, you will find that the two working together will run the picture up to even a greater cost, for each one of them will do certain pet scenes, and whatever way they divide the scenes each will try to outdo the other, and the result will be double effort and double the cost to the picture. When they worked for the Triangle Studio, they started there as errand boys, Mr. Woods of the Triangle Co. ruled them with an iron hand. Unless you do likewise, you have not got a Chinaman's chance.

I am now giving you full power to take such action as you deem necessary to protect the Fox Film Corporation against any one man who is supposedly working for the Fox Film Corporation and receiving his salary, but all the time is working for himself, and not thinking of the concern that is paying him.

You know the limit to be expended on pictures made in Los Angeles, and I look to you to see that this is carried out.

Very truly yours,
(signed) William Fox

New York City
February 16, 1918

Mr. S.M. Wurtzel
Los Angeles

My dear Sol:

I have your letter of January 31st, your #44*; I have carefully read its contents, and I have reviewed the picture *The Girl with the Champagne Eyes*.

I fully agree with you that there is nothing contained in this story that should have cost over $15,000; in fact, under the favorable conditions existing in California, it should have been produced for less than that, having in mind the person playing the leading part got a nominal salary. I fully agree with the plan in your mind, not to permit this man to direct another picture, and that we await the action of the Government in the present Draft, to see whether or not he will be take. If he is drafted, that of course, terminates his written contract with us. If, when the Draft is announced, he is not taken, then I will advise you what further action to take. If, in the meantime, you think that he can be of any help to his brother, rather than have him sit around doing nothing, assign him to work with his brother, however, with the distinct understanding that you have absolute control, and that if, at the conclusion of the picture that his brother is making, you find you have no control of him either, and that he is not working in accordance with the views you have in mind, you will likewise not permit him to start photographing his next picture, and I will then give you advice as to what action to take with reference to both of these gentlemen.

In my opinion, the disturbing factor with the Franklins is McConville (Bernard), the scenario writer. His contract expires on March 12th. I am of the opinion that "the can should be tied" to him. You will have no difficulty in replacing him at the salary he is getting. I think he is disturbing the minds of these two boys and therefore, after March 12th, he is no longer to remain in the employ of the Company, and I suggest that you immediately secure a first class and high grade scenario writer to take his place.

The above opinion of McConville was formed by me when I was still in Los Angeles. For instance, while I was there, he saw fit to walk into a set that had been properly dressed by our Construction Dept., and found fault with the equipment. It was necessary for me to call him into the office and tell him that his duty was to economize for the Company and not to disturb the director, and he had no right and it was not his place to criticize any set. He promised me he would not do it again. While he many not have done it publicly, I do not think he carried out his promise, and it is my opinion that he at all time is the instigator of the troubles with the Franklins. Therefore, as I said above, he should be let out after the termination of his present contract, which according to my understanding, expires on March 12th.

*For easier reference, the two correspondents numbered many of their letters.

Very truly yours,
(signed) William Fox

Los Angeles
February 26, 1918

(COPY)
Mr. William Fox
OUR LETTER NO. 65
New York City

My dear Mr. Fox:

I wish to acknowledge your letter of February 16th, which was in reply to my letter No. 44.

I note what you say about Chet Franklin and the draft. I have asked Alfred Wright, our attorney, to try to see if he could find out when the next draft would be called. He made inquiry and found that it was impossible to know just when this may take place. It may take place within the next month, and it might not take place until next June. I am writing you again about this, because I don't know whether you would want to keep Chet Franklin on the payroll as long as June first, or later if the draft should not be called then.

With reference to having Chet Franklin help his brother, I have gone into this very carefully and have come to the conclusion that it would be impractical to do this; as, in my opinion, Chet Franklin would be a hindrance more than a help. I am, therefore, having him do nothing until I get further word from you. I am having no trouble whatsoever now with Sid Franklin, and he is doing his work in accordance with my views.

With reference to McConville, the scenario writer, I was under the impression that I had written you what action I had taken with reference to him, but, on looking over my correspondence, I find that I failed to do so. When I disbanded the Chet Franklin company, I called McConville into my office and gave him fifteen minutes to get off the lot. I figured that we would be far better off and would be saving money to pay McConville his salary up to the finish of his contract and not have him around.

You are correct in stating that one of the main causes as to why we have had trouble with the Franklins is McConville. I also let out the cutter who the Franklins had — a girl by the name of Della Conley — so that now the only people remaining of the two Franklin companies are Sid Franklin and his assistant, Ward Lascelle. All the other people in Sid Franklin's company are new people.

Respectfully yours,
Sol M. Wurtzel

New York City
March 4, 1918

Mr. S.M. Wurtzel
Los Angeles

My dear Sol:

The pleasure of playing *Cleopatra* the third week in San Francisco cost us $521 which we are now subtracting from the profits of the first two weeks.

Very truly yours,
(signed) William Fox

Helen Gardner's Cleopatra *had proved to be such a success when it was made in 1912 that the Fox company decided to make their own version in 1917. Directed by J. Gordon Edwards, it was a lavish spectacle in ten parts and starred Theda Bara with the renowned actor Fritz Leiber as Julius Caesar, and Thurston Hall as Anthony. The reviews agreed that Bara made a daring display of her physical charms but that the mob scenes with thousands of extras were not handled with the mastery of Griffith. The script was described as a literary patchwork of Shakespeare, Sardou and the scenario writer, Adrean Johnson.*

The Fox Corporation's 1917 version suffered rough going similar to that of its successor's notorious version of the sixties, but it eventually made a million dollars.

Wurtzel must have felt responsible for advising an extended run in San Francisco for he noted on the margin of his boss's sarcastic letter that the epic had lost $294.55 as the result of its three week run in the Bay City.

New York City
March 12, 1918

Mr. S.M. Wurtzel

My dear Sol:

The following wire came from Sid Franklin today: "Considering that I expected a wire from you congratulating me upon turning out a record picture as to time and cost without the ear marks of speed and economy I was surprised at the letter received by Mr. Wurtzel. Miss Carmen endeavoring to assist Schumway in negligee should only be construed in one way eagerness to assist the son of her benefactor partly forgetful of self. Greater liberties as to reputation have been taken in life and pictures by girls endeavoring to aid unfortunates. The girl realizing her mistake and her pity turning to hate and fear when Schumway kisses her. It is not wrong in Carmen refusing to kiss the crook as the characterization of the crook was

that of lustfulness from the start of the story instinctively turning her gratitude to hate. The criticism of direction in reference to these situations are
erroneous and at worse can only be termed difference of opinion and those
favoring my opinion will mention Mr. Wurtzel who passed on story and
picture and Gordon Edwards who passed favorably on finished production.
While it is your privilege to cut pictures to suite yourself I frankly state
that in making the cuts you mentioned you have removed some of the best
and most entertaining points. My attitude is that of cooperation as you can
see by the cost of my last picture in response to your request for cheaper
production. I await your wire."

The following wire was received from you today. "Received your letter March sixth reference Carmen picture *Bride of Fear*— If prints have
not yet been made I beg you to please withhold making changes mentioned in your letter until you receive my letter of today written after
conference with Gordon Edwards who reviewed picture with me before it
was shipped New York."

Of course, I am not interested in the comment Franklin makes, nor
am I interested in the comment you make. The final judgment with reference to any picture made by the Fox Film Corporation, you ought to
know, is left with me and not with you or Mr. Franklin. I am awfully
sorry you saw fit to wire me or write a letter or discuss it with Mr.
Franklin, which cause him to send the wire he did. You know my practice here in New York. You know that there never was a scene that I ever
cut out of a picture that met with the director's approval. Each director
thinks the scenes he photographs are the most wonderful in the world,
and I never followed the policy of consulting a director when I thought a
scene should be eliminated. If I had done that, the Fox Film Corporation
would have been on the rocks long ago. The only reason the Fox Film
Corporation has made progress is because the power as to what will or
will not remain in the film, has been entirely left with me, and I have
used it in such a way as to make possible the progress of the Fox Film
Corporation. I am not interested in any further controversy in this matter. My sentiments as expressed in my previous letter, are stronger today
than they were then, and I do not want any further controversy or correspondence on the matter. This matter is now closed. You are to blame for
it being necessary for me to write this note. However, as I said before,
this matter, so far as I am concerned, is entirely closed.

Very truly yours.
(signed) William Fox

Over the years Sol Wurtzel developed chronic constipation and a facial tic that curled the side of his mouth into a nervous smile. From the events that followed one after another in 1918, it is easy to see why these afflictions developed.

Theda Bara — the sexy vamp with the exotic background, was strictly a creation of clever Fox press-agentry but it didn't take too long the Theodosia Goodman, the proper Jewish girl from Cincinnati, to believe every word of it. Her indignation crackled across the wires when her plebeian beginnings were exposed in a Cleveland newspaper interview given by Abe Carlos. Fox, who had the cagey habit of saying he was out of town whenever he wanted to avoid an annoying situation, tried the dodge again but he forgot that Wurtzel had once been his private secretary.

WESTERN UNION TELEGRAM (copy)

Los Angeles
March 12, 1918

MR. WILLIAM FOX
NEW YORK CITY

Bara showed me article which appeared in recent issue of the "Cleveland News" to the effect that Carlos in an interview made following statement — Carlos discovered Bara at Churchill's and engaged her for *A Fool There Was* at thirty dollars per week mentioning her as being a Churchill acquaintance — also made statement concerning her engagement in "Kruetzer's Sonata" and remarks said to have been made by Brennon (Herbert — director) before she was engaged for this part — Miss Bara is in a condition of mind now owing to this article where she doesn't want to finish "*Salome*" and demands that Carlos makes a retraction — she has personally telegraphed to the Cleveland News demanding retraction and denial of statements contained in article.

Sol M. Wurtzel

WESTERN UNION TELEGRAM

New York City
March 14, 1918

Sol M. Wurtzel
Los Angeles

Received your telegram March 12. Mr. Fox has been out of city past two weeks on account of ill health and expects to return in about week or ten days. Will refer your telegram to him immediately upon his return.

M.L. PINCUS

WESTERN UNION TELEGRAM (copy)

Los Angeles
March 15, 1918

MR. M.L. PINCUS
NEW YORK CITY

My wire of March twelfth is of such a nature I think you should call to Mr. Fox's attention immediately.

Sol M. Wurtzel

WESTERN UNION TELEGRAM (handwritten copy)

Mr. Winfield Sheehan
Fox Film Co.

Slanderous interview credited to Carlos printed in Cleveland paper. Demand instant retraction if he made statements or denial of having made them if he claims he did not. Most insulting innuendo I ever read. Wire from Pincus say Mr. Fox is out of town so will expect to hear from you. You will understand that this matter cannot admit of delay as it emanated from a Fox Film employee. Am awaiting your answer and know you will see to this personally.

Theda Bara

The slanderous interview by the photoplay editor of the Cleveland News *insinuated that Bara might have been an employee rather than a guest at Churchill's.*
Since Churchill's was a very fashionable restaurant in Manhattan where only the "best" people went to dine and dance, one wonders why the temperamental beauty was so outraged. As the editor wrote: "Any young woman who can increase her weekly salary from $30.00 to $5000.00 in the short space of three years is deserving of modicum of credit — even a vamp."

No sooner was Bara quieted down than private detectives were put on the trail of the beautiful blonde ingenue — Jewel Carmen. Photoplay *magazine described her as a lovely, luscious blonde who was a naive convent school girl when discovered by Douglas Fairbanks. Her Mary Pickford-like aura was strictly for the camera though and off the set she caused Wurtzel headaches aplenty.*

SPECIAL REPORT

LOS ANGELES OPERATING #1788
LOS ANGELES INVESTIGATOR #23 REPORTS:

Los Angeles
Wed. April 3rd, 1918

At 1:30 PM I was instructed by Manager G.P.P. to accompany Investigator #9 to the Fox Film Company and to report to Mr. Wurtzel for information and data relative to work he wished done.

On arrival we met Mr. Wurtzel and Mr. Seiler and they advised us that June (Jewel) Carmen had drawn $250.00 advance on salary March 22nd, stating that her mother was undergoing an operation and she wished an advance to meet the expenses. They have not seen or heard from her since and have been unable to get any definite information from her people or friends as to where she is. They gave us her home address and also of a friend of hers and any information they could.

After receiving the above Investigator #9 and I called at her home 4118 Hollywood Boulevard where under a pretext we interviewed her sister and after some explaining and persuasion she stated that her sister was hiding in New York at the present time from the Fox Film Company. She also exhibited a telegram from her sister stating that she was leaving New York City Friday for home.

We immediately returned to the Fox Film Company and reported the result to Mr. Seiler and returning to the Agency at 4 PM discontinued.

EXPENSES:	Carfare	$ .10
Time:	One-half day	$4.00
Total		$4.10

SPECIAL REPORT

LOS ANGELES OPERATING #1788
LOS ANGELES INVESTIGATOR #9 REPORTS:

Los Angeles
Wed., April 3rd 1918

At 1:30 PM I was instructed to go to the Fox Film Company 1400 North Western Avenue and there interview the client regarding the above matter.

I immediately left the offices of the Agency in company with Investigator #23 and we went to the client's place of business via the street car where we arrived a 2 PM. We were conducted to the client on the lot where he told us what he wished to ascertain and gave us the address of the subject's mother and sister and the name of a girl friend of hers from whom we might learn something of value.

Leaving the Client we proceeded to the home of the subject's mother and sister at 5118 Hollywood Boulevard and found the subject's sister lives in Apartment #2. This informant came to the small balcony over-head and at first told me the subject was in San Diego but she could not give us her address there. We used a suitable pretext and finally got the woman to come down stairs. Here she told us that her sister, the subject, was remaining in hiding for business reasons, and that she did not wish anyone to know her address. I told this informant that it would be to the subject's interest to let me get in communication with her at once and the subject's sister finally told me that as long as I did not come from the client she would tell me and upon the assurance that I did not she stated that her sister is now in New York City and is stopping at the Wentworth Hotel and 46th Street.

She also showed us a telegram from the subject which she stated she had received yesterday which read that the subject would leave for Los Angeles Friday sure. My informant told us that she did not believe the subject had made any new connections and that she had to be back here Tuesday next. Fearing to excite suspicion I did not ask why the subject had gone to New York but from what her sister said I am of the opinion it was for business reasons.

We returned to the client's place of business and reported the fore-going to him and then returned to the office of the agency where we arrived at 4 PM and discontinued for the day.

EXPENSES:	Carfare	$ .10
Time	½ day	$4.00
Total		$4.10

The beautiful and unreliable Carmen returned to make another picture but another new set of problems arose featuring director Frank Lloyd and his friend, actor William Farnum. Farnum at this time was the most popular male star Fox Films had under contract. His weekly salary ran into the thousands while Tom Mix's was still in the hundreds, and his home and mode of living was amongst the most lavish in Hollywood.

With his rugged good looks and debonair manner, "Bill" Farnum brought a rich background of stage experience to the screen. He was a good Shakespearean actor who was both a matinee idol and robust he-man — a magic combination at the box-office. William Fox held him in high personal regard and nothing was too good for him at either coast. He was starred in such outstanding classics as Tale of Two Cities, Les Misérables, *and with his brother Dustin,* The Corsican Brothers. *His current assignment was Zane Grey's* Riders of the Purple Sage.

WESTERN UNION TELEGRAM (copy)

Los Angeles
May 23, 1918

MR. WILLIAM FOX

Frank Lloyd returned Tuesday from Arizona with company and is now making finishing scenes and some retakes of *Riders of Purple Sage*— through an unfortunate accident scenes that Lloyd photographed one day in Grand Canyon were fogged — Lloyd insists on going back to Grand Canyon to retake these scenes which could mean an expenditure figuring salaries of company and star of about six thousand dollars— in my opinion these scenes do not affect the continuity or dramatic action of picture and are on the scenic effect.

Lloyd says that if picture not necessary for immediate release he could retake scenes when he goes to Grand Canyon in about three weeks to make scenes for *Rainbow Trail* but that if picture is needed immediately he will not want picture shipped to New York unless the scenes are included — Lloyd also insists on sample prints being made in Los Angeles— this will mean several days delay in shipping picture — I also had talk with Lloyd regarding cost of *Rainbow Trail*— Lloyd says the minimum cost of this picture without star's salary would be thirty thousand and would probably cost thirty-five and would photograph picture in four weeks— since Farnum came to Los Angeles Frank Lloyd has been a different man — before that he was working for the interest of the company now he is working only for himself and for Farnum — he has become arrogant, vain and impossible to talk to— he has many times intimated to me that unless pictures he direct are released as shipped from Los Angeles he would quit — he has told me he was dissatisfied with the way picture *Blindness of Divorce* was titled and edited — he has told me that in all probability he would only make two or three more pictures for company— he also told me that company could afford to make expensive pictures with Farnum without incurring loss and that flattering offers are continually being made to him.

Lloyd's stand is practically that unless he is allowed to make pictures as he wants to without interference he would rather quit — I do not know how Farnum figures in on this but I am morally certain that he is back of Lloyd — all my talks with Lloyd have been diplomatic and I have not tried to force an issue — I am taking this up by telegraph because Lloyd will finish photographing in studio end of this week and will be ready to start on *Rainbow Trail* unless he goes back to Grand Canyon now to make retakes— will you please wire me whether you want Lloyd to make retakes in Grand Canyon now? Also if he should go ahead on *Rainbow Trail* at cost he estimates. Also what action I should take in case he refuses to abide by your decisions—cost of *Riders of Purple Sage*, if Lloyd does not retake canyon scene now will be approximately eighty-five thousand including Farnum's salary.

SOL M. WURTZEL

WESTERN UNION TELEGRAM

New York City
May 24, 1918

S M Wurtzel
Los Angeles

Conference with Edwards he has my wire. Show him wire you sent to me then report by wire result. By all means try and save the retaining of scenes. Cost of picture at present far in excess of our ability to receive in rentals. Show this wire also to Edwards.

WILLIAM FOX

Los Angeles
May 28, 1918

Mr. William Fox

My dear Mr. Fox:

With reference to my telegram to you of May 23rd regarding Frank Lloyd, I received in reply your telegram of May 24th, and Gordon Edwards showed me your telegram to him.

Mr. Edwards has been fully aware of this entire matter from the beginning, and I have often consulted with him on it. Before sending you my telegram of May 23rd, I showed it to Mr. Edwards and he advised me to send it in view of Lloyd's attitude.

When Lloyd came to Los Angeles last October and made the *Kingdom of Love* with Carmen, he worked heart and soul for the company, as the pictures showed when finished. He was also a great help to me in getting matters straightened out. However, the minute Farnum stepped off the train last February, Lloyd was a different man, and he has since been a different man.

He has become vain, arrogant, and it is impossible to talk to him. His entire staff have taken the same attitude, refusing to abide by the rules of the studio. The result has been a waste of time and money, which was apparent in *True Blue* and the *Riders of the Purple Sage*.

Many times Lloyd has told me he would quit unless pictures he directed were released exactly as they were shipped from Los Angeles, and that he would write you to that effect. He is always complaining that he is doing the company a favor by working for it for his present salary as he has been offered double the money, also that he has received offers to make pictures for independent concerns at $150,000 each.

He did not mention with who he was to make them, but I presume with Farnum. His attitude therefore, is that the Fox Film Corporation can afford to spend $100,00 on each Farnum picture without incurring a loss, and he has expressed this to me. He also told me that in all probability he would only make two or three more pictures for the company and then quit.

Lloyd knows exactly what sum should be expended for the Farnum pictures, for I have often taken it up with him and told him your views. He also knows what expense it is to each Farnum picture if we have long delays between pictures. Dustin Farnum is now making pictures for the Sherman Film Company, and they are making eight reel productions; the one they just finished The *Light of the Western Stars* by Zane Gray, I understand cost $90,00. The conclusion I draw is, that William Farnum and Frank Lloyd want their picture to cost as much.

When Lloyd began making *True Blue*, he began showing his present spirit. I tried to show him where he was making a mistake, and he said he would quit unless I did not interfere with him. He apologized later, but did not change his methods.

When Lloyd returned from Arizona, some scenes that he photographed in one day in the Grand Canyon, through an unfortunate accident were fogged in our laboratory. Lloyd immediately said he would go back to the Grand Canyon, although he knew the scenes that were spoiled were not action scenes, and would not affect the drama or continuity of the picture, being merely scenic shots, and that to go back just for one day's work would mean a cost of about $7000. In view of the stand he took, also in view of the fact he said the *Rainbow Trail* could not be made for less than $30,000 (without Farnum's salary), I thought it best to advise you of the entire situation. I first consulted with Edwards about it, and he agreed with me.

When I received your telegram of May 24th, I again had a talk with Lloyd; he still insisted that if the picture was to be released now he would go back to retake the scenes. I therefore told him the picture would not be released at this time, and he could retake the scenes when he goes back to the Grand Canyon to make his exteriors for the *Rainbow Trail*. He finally agreed to this, and an extra print will be made so he can insert the missing scenes and send it to you so corrections could be made in the negative. Lloyd said he would not trust the New York office in anything for they were ruining all his pictures.

I am of the firm opinion that Lloyd will never again make a Farnum picture at a reasonable cost; and in my opinion if it can be arranged, Mr. LeSaint should direct Farnum after the *Rainbow Trail* and Lloyd should direct Brockwell. Will you be good enough to let me know your ideas on this, and if you approve of it.

Very truly yours,
Sol M. Wurtzel

New York City
June 7, 1918

Mr. Sol M. Wurtzel
Los Angeles

My dear Sol:

I wish to acknowledge receipt of your letter of May 28th. Your situation is so complicated that I really don't know what to say. From your letter it is evident that you infer that Farnum and Lloyd have a complete understanding which I hardly believe is possible, but if they have an understanding how can you possibly arrange for LeSaint to direct Farnum? If you can arrange it I have no objection.

Lloyd, as you know, has a written contract with our Company and if it can be arranged for Farnum to work with LeSaint, Mr. Lloyd will have to carry out his contract with us whether he like it or not. I would be very sorry to see a disagreement between Lloyd and the Fox Film Corporation, for I have a high personal regard for him. I would consider that he is acting dirty and mean if he did anything to disturb the condition of the Fox Film Corporation.

It is because of the above that I am unable to give you advice in the matter. However, if you can arrange to have LeSaint direct Farnum, why do it. It appears to me that I am unable to be of assistance in this matter by letter writing, that to straighten this matter out it would necessitate my going to Los Angeles, which at this time I am unable and unwilling to do; therefore I would advise you in a tactful and diplomatic way to straighten out your differences.

By the way — what have you decided for Farnum's next story, after *The Rainbow Trail*? I am in hope that by the time you receive this letter your differences will be entirely straightened out to the satisfaction of everyone. If not, however, take it up with me again.

For your information, I wish to advise you that we have postponed the release of *Riders of the Purple Sage* until September. This is for your confidential information. I feel that there should not be that gap that there would be between *The Riders of the Purple Sage*, now we would not release *The Rainbow Trail* until September, and I wanted them both finished so that I could see them both before I released either one.

I again want to repeat that I think Edwards in his usual diplomatic way could get at the bottom of the trouble and could very easily find out just what the difficulty is, and I also want to say that if you can arrange with Farnum that LeSaint should direct him, which I have serious doubts you will be able to do, why then Mr. Lloyd will be obliged to take our orders and will be obliged to conduct himself in a manner satisfactory to the Fox Film Corporation. I however, would be very sorry to use any compulsory methods in straightening this matter out. I am in hopes that either you or Edwards can do it in a diplomatic quiet way. The thing that will help you greatly will be that my efforts in the last Drive* and the result of this Sales Convention have laid me up. If you can diplomatically spread that rumor into Farnum's ear, you will find that he will stand by me. If you told him that you are unwilling to annoy me, that you have heard from member of my family that I am in a condition of health where I must not be aggravated or annoyed, this might be the diplomatic way of getting out of it.

I am in the same mail writing to Farnum informing him of my breakdown so that it will help you along and so that when you speak to him about the condition of my health it won't be news to him.

Very truly yours.
(signed) William Fox

WESTERN UNION TELEGRAM

New York City
June 12, 1918

Sol Wurtzel
Los Angeles

Have you shipped *Riders of the Purple Sage*— have you decided on story after *Rainbow Trail*— I am still of opinion Pierre Legrand great story — is there likelihood of you engaging immediately director for George Walsh? If so will send him to you.

William Fox

New York City

Fox was chairman of the Theatrical & Motion Picture Committee of the United War Work Campaign Fund Drive.

June 12, 1918

Mr. S.M. Wurtzel

My dear Sol:

I am just writing these few lines to set forth the new policy of the Fox Film Corp. as agreed on at the fourth annual Convention. This is for your confidential information and is not to be discussed by you with anyone.

First: Twenty-six (26) Standard Pictures to be made up as follows: If possible, eight Farnums, 8 Baras, and 10 special pictures, 4 of which we have already laid plans for and one of which we have entirely completed, the second partly completed. The completed one is made by Raoul Walsh entitled *Know Your Enemy*. The one partly completed is being made by Stanton* based on the life of General Pershing. Raoul Walsh will make the next story from a book by Theodore Roosevelt *On the Firing Line*. Stanton's next story is a propaganda story which we have not named as yet. Our plans are that all of these four pictures will be ready for release by the 1st of September. Our further plans are to continue Stanton and Walsh in making this special type of story to be released under Standard heading.

While on this point, I wanted to say to you, in reply to your letter with reference to the director† who made *The Garden of Allah* and *The Spoilers*, that if perchance there is submitted to you any especially large stories which can be made for about $50,000 or less without a star, however a story that has special advertising value, big enough to attract people to the box office without have a star, and a production that will have great merit, the story to be based on a topic that is of vital interest to the public at this time (for example *The Blindness of Divorce* or one like *The Cailleaux Case* which we have made and not yet released)— if such material is submitted to you and the director who made *The Garden of Allah* and *The Spoilers* is still available, it would be agreeable to me for you to made two or three such pictures a season. Of course, it is not always the expensive production that goes— for example, *The Beasts of Berlin* could never have cost over $15.000 and DID not take over three weeks to photograph, but was so timely as to warrant the special attention of the public all over the world.

The type of picture that is made by Lois Weber‡ which the Universal people release in a special way, is what I have in mind, however ours to be a more pretentious production than they usually make, but based on a vitally important subject that is being discussed universally. This is not to

*Richard Stanton-Director. †Colin Campbell. ‡First woman producer and director.

be started by you immediately. You may take your time and you will first submit to me the material that you think will make that type of story before you make arrangements, for these stories under the STANDARD heading will have to be well planned, well mapped out, and agreed on here in New York before I want you to decide on any picture that will go in under that heading. I am simply sending you this word by way of suggestion, so that you may have in mind what kind and type of pictures will be wanted in Standard Pictures.

Second: A second brand of pictures of which we intend making twenty (26) will be the Victory Brand. In this brand will be George Walsh, Tom Mix, and a woman whom we have not as yet decided upon, a woman who must be of especial merit and value and who has a splendid reputation, and for whose services the Fox Film Corporation would be willing to pay a handsome price, if she were the woman that all our exchanges would agree on as having special value in their territory. We are searching for such a woman here in New York. You can make a search in Los Angeles, although I know of no one who is there who would fit this program. It is intended to have 26 pictures with these three stars. The brand will be known as Victory Brand. I want you to make every effort to make the Tom Mix pictures splendid and vital, for I think he is on the road of a sure fire if we just pay attention to him. I have wired you this day inquiring whether you can find a high class director for George Walsh, one who could control him and one who is big enough mentally to make good pictures with him.

Third: The third brand will be the X-L Brand, in which Gladys Brockwell, Jewel Carmen, and Virginia Pearson will appear. There will be twenty-six (26) pictures with these three stars. This last brand would be the type of picture that we would sell at the same price as we are now selling the 52 special a years, and which is the class of picture on which we do not want the cost to run more than from fifteen to eighteen thousand dollars. Of course, it is our intention to make the Victory Brand so as not to cost any more than that, if it can possibly be done, which will enable the Fox Film Corporation to sell these pictures at a fair profit. However, in the case of the Victory Brand, rather than sacrifice the story, it will be agreeable to spend a limited additional amount of money, so long as it would be an exceptional production.

The purpose of having these three brands is to make it possible for the stars to become popular enough in the X-L Brand to advance them to the Victory Brand and those in the Victory Brand to advance them to Standard Pictures, so that at all times we will be making a brand of film in which to popularize new people. If this plan works out successfully we will at all times be protected against each brand of film, for just as we could popularize people in the X-L brand to make them fitted for the Victory Brand, so could we popularize those in the Victory Brand to put them into Standard Pictures, and if God forbid, anything happened to any of our stars in the first two brands, we would have sufficient strength to move one to the other, so as not to cripple or hurt the Fox Film Corporation.

This note is written to you for the following reasons:

1st: For your private information

2nd: For your consideration of a special director of extraordinary merit to make extraordinary pictures, without stars, to be classed in Standard Pictures

3rd: For your guidance with reference to pictures in the X-L Brand.

4th: For your guidance with reference to pictures in the Victory Brand.

I am anxiously awaiting the arrival of *Salome*, also *Riders of the Purple Sage*. I am also awaiting word from you as to whether your next Farnum story, after *Rainbow Trail*, has been agreed upon, so that there is no time lost between *Rainbow Trail* and the following story.

Now that drives have come to an end and I have a little time to myself to attend to business, I expect to sit down to write you at great length within the course of next week, a complete review of all pictures made by you since my last review. In the meantime, I want to say that I am highly pleased with your conduct, and I look forward to great results through your efforts.

> With kindest regards, I am
> Very truly yours,
> (signed) William Fox

WESTERN UNION TELEGRAM (copy)

> Los Angeles
> June 13, 1918

Mr. William Fox
New York City

We are cutting negative *Riders of Purple Sage* will positively ship same by June twenty first — Farnum and Lloyd don't like *Pierre Legrande*— have in preparation *Sea Story* which will be Farnum's next after *Rainbow Trail*— have assigned writer Charles Kenyon to Lloyd company to prepare stories for William Farnum — director Cliff Smith has just finished picture for Triangle. I consider him good man for George Walsh. Salary three hundred fifty is ready to begin immediately if satisfactory. Will appreciate wire from you by Saturday as Smith would like immediate answer.

SOL M. WURTZEL

WESTERN UNION TELEGRAM

New York City
June 14, 1918

SM WURTZEL
LOS ANGELES

You failed to give names of any pictures Cliff Smith directed there-fore unable to give you decision — before sending Walsh to Los Angeles I naturally want to see pictures of the director you recommend. Telegraph list immediately.

WILLIAM FOX

WESTERN UNION (copy)

June 14, 1918

MR. WILLIAM FOX
NEW YORK CITY

Cliff Smith directed all Roy Stewart pictures for Triangle. I have it on good authority he was allowed eighteen days to make each picture. Two latest pictures were *Boss of the Lazy Y* and *Faith Endurin.*

SOL M. WURTZEL

Los Angeles
June 17, 1918

Mr. William Fox

My dear Mr. Fox:

I wish to acknowledge receipt of your letter of June 7th which was in reply to my letter of May 28th regarding Frank Lloyd and William Farnum. I have very carefully noted what you say, and I am glad to be able to write you that at this time my difference with Lloyd have been straightened out, and everything is going along very nicely, and I hope and will do my best to see that it continues that way and that I will not have occasion to write you again about it.

Regarding Farnum's next story, as I wired you on June 13th, I have assigned writer Charles Kenyon to Farnum, and He is now preparing a *Sea Story,* which we have decided on will be Farnum's next. I took up the story of *Pierre Le Grande* again with Lloyd, also with Farnum and they both are of the opinion that it is not suitable for Farnum. Therefore, for the time being I will keep it in reserve.

Farnum and Lloyd told me that after doing the sea story, they would like to do some well know classic, like *The Corsican Brothers*, or some other book, uncopywrited, like *Tale of Two Cities* or *Les Miserables*, Farnum says that he has spoken to you several times about *The Corsican Brothers* and he would like your opinion on it; or if you can suggest some other well known classic that you would like to have him do. The New York office has better facilities for looking up such material than we have here, and we would all appreciate suggestions from you and decide on one soon, so that we could make our plans and get ready with sets, etc., ahead of time.

I note what you say about the release of *Riders of the Purple Sage* and *Rainbow Trail*. The *Riders of the Purple Sage* will be shipped by the end of this week. Lloyd has been photographing The *Rainbow Trail* the past week and is making good progress on it. Under separate cover I mailed you a copy of the scenario.

At the present time LeSaint is working on the story *Kultur* and will finish photographing by the end of this week. I am sure that this will turn out to be a first class Brockwell picture.

Reynolds* began photographing today on a new Mix picture, *Mysterious Logan*, and judging from the scenario, which I have mailed you under separate cover, it should turn out to be as good as the previous Mix pictures.

Thornby[†] has finished photographing *You Can't Get Away with It*, with Jewel Carmen. It is now in the cutting room, and will be shipped in a few days. Thornby was handicapped somewhat owing to Miss Carmen being ill; he will begin photographing the next picture in a few days, the story being *Above the Law* which was purchased in New York.

J. Gordon Edwards has taken up with you direct by wire regarding the future plans for Bara. He finishes photographing *The Message of the Lilies* today, and his next story with Miss Bara will be *The Wildcat*, a story which we just purchased here. A copy of the scenario will be mailed you in a few days, it is now being written. The story *The Light* which was purchased in New York, Edwards will reserve, and will do it later with her.

Everything is going along splendidly at the studios; I am trying hard to get together a good scenario staff so that we will be able to take care of the other companies you will send out here later.

Very truly yours,

Los Angeles
June 21, 1918
Our Letter No. 125

*Lynn Reynolds — director. [†]Robert Thornby — director

(copy)
Mr. William Fox
New York City

My dear Mr. Fox:

I wish to acknowledge your letter of June 12th with reference to the plans of the Fox Film Corporation for the next season. I have read and gone over your letter very carefully.

I have your telegram of June 20th, which read as follows:

"Looked at feature Smith directed not satisfied — he would not be the man for George Walsh — therefore make further search — under present plans George Walsh would reach Los Angeles by August tenth this will give you sufficient time to find proper director and proper vehicle."

I am not at all surprised that you were not satisfied with the pictures you saw that Cliff Smith directed. I, myself, did not consider them high-class pictures; however, I took into consideration the conditions under which this director worked at the Triangle Studio. He made one picture every three weeks; he was given a scenario, and he was not allowed to change one single scene in the entire script.

The Triangle system was, for the manager, who at that time was Ho.O. Davis, to give all directors instructions as to what they were to do the following day, what scenes they were to photograph; where to go for locations, etc. Taking all these things into consideration, I felt that Smith did good work, and that, if allowed leeway and if he worked under our methods, he would prove to be a good director for us. I wish to call to your attention that Lynn Reynolds came to us from Triangle, and that the pictures he directed for Triangle were on par with Cliff Smith's pictures; but I felt that Reynolds had merit which showed in spite of the system under which he worked. The same is true of LeSaint, who came to us from Universal. It is a well known fact around Los Angeles studios that LeSaint never made a good picture in his life before he came with the Fox Film Corporation — simply because he never had a chance when he worked for Universal and Lasky. I have met with director Cliff Smith and have great confidence in him and I am sure that, if he were to come with us, he would turn out meritorious pictures. I originally had Smith in mind for Tom Mix when we were looking for a director for him before we engaged Reynolds, but, at that time Smith was tied up; however I will abide by your decision in the matter, and will look around for another director for George Walsh.

I am going to make a change in directors with Jewel Carmen and Tom Mix at the conclusion of their present pictures. At the present time Lynn Reynolds is directing Tom Mix and Robert Thornby is directing

Jewel Carmen. Reynolds has always expressed a desire and a preference to direct a woman, and as Tom Mix is satisfied to have Thornby, I am going to make the change; so, at the end of their present pictures, Thornby will direct Mix and Reynolds will direct Carmen. As both of these directors will finish their present pictures about the same time, no loss of time will result by make the change.

I wish to acknowledge receipt of your telegram of congratulation on *Salome* for which I sincerely thank you. I also wish to sincerely thank you for your kind works of appreciation, which will only make me work for better and greater results in the future.

With kindest regards, I am
Respectfully yours,

SPECIAL REPORT

Los Angeles Operating #1844
Los Angeles Investigator #9 Reports

Los Angeles
(Thursday) July 11, 1918

At 3:30 PM, Manager G.P.P. instructed me in company with Investigator #109 to endeavor to ascertain the present whereabouts of Jewel Carmen. Owing to the lateness of the hour and her residence being at such a distance from the office of the agency we hired an auto and proceeded to this address.

On arriving there and ringing the bell and receiving no response thereto I tried the lower door found it unlocked. I went to the top of the stairs where I rapped on the inner door and owing to no response I tried the door again and found it unlocked. I opened same and looked in. The apartment was unoccupied with the exception of a white Persian cat asleep on the couch.

At the same time that I was endeavoring to get a response to the ringing of the doorbell a bill collector was also endeavoring to get in communication with the subject. He stated to me that he had made numerous calls on the subject but was unable to get any response. He also informed me he had entered the apartment but could find no one in. He further stated that she had owed this account long before she went to New York before and that it was almost impossible to collect on them.

We remained in this vicinity until 6 PM but owing to the lateness of the hour the pretext I had selected to use could not be used. We were then driven to the Sal Lake Station where our machine was dismissed and a search of the record made there. We also went to the Santa Fe ticket office and searched their record, but with no success. I then boarded a car going to the Southern Pacific Ticket Office where we failed to find any record of a ticket having been sold to Jewel Carmen.

I then boarded a car and returned to 5118 Hollywood Blvd. but up until 8 PM their apartment was in darkness and I was unable to get any response to the ringing of the door bell.

I then boarded a car and returned to my home where I discontinued at 9 PM.

	EXPENSES:	Auto Hire	$ 4.00
		Carfare	$ .20
		Dinner	$ .75
		Total	$ 4.95
	TIME:	One day	$ 8.00
			$12.95

SPECIAL REPORT

LOS ANGELES OPERATING #1844
LOS ANGELES INVESTIGATOR #109 REPORTS:

Los Angeles
Friday, July 12, 1918

Continuing on the above case I left the Agency Office at 8:30 AM and boarded a car for Hollywood arriving there at 9:15 AM and proceeded to the residence of Jewel Carmen. I rang the door repeatedly but to no avail.

I stayed in the vicinity of this place until 11 AM at which time I again tried to raise someone at her residence but again met with failure. I then boarded a car and went to the office of Manager G.P.P. where I reported.

While waiting to accompany Manager G.P.P. to Mr. Wurtzel's office where we reported to him and after a conference it was decided to place said residence under surveillance. Accordingly I met investigator #140 at 2 PM and together we proceeded to the vicinity of the residence in question.

On arrival at 2:30 PM we took up the surveillance of the house. At 7:30 PM an automobile, Hup. No. 358838 drove up in front of the residence and three women and a young man got out and entered the apartment. Shortly after the Investigator #140 called under pretext to interview the subject if possible but was unsuccessful. At 10:15 PM a young fellow and a brunette came out and entered the car and drove towards Los Angles.

We continued the surveillance until 11 PM at which time we boarded a car for our residences and discontinued for the day at 12 midnight.

EXPENSES: Lunch in Hollywood $ .50

	Supper	$ .75
	Carfare	$ .25
	Total	$1.50
TIME:	One day	$8.00
		$9.50

WESTERN UNION TELEGRAM

New York City
July 12, 1918

SOL WURTZEL
LOS ANGELES

I am informed Jewel Carmen is in New York — has she left the studio and if so wire me why she left to my home in Hewlett Bay Park Long Island.

WILLIAM FOX

SPECIAL REPORT

LOS ANGELES OPERATING #1844
LOS ANGELES INVESTIGATOR #109 REPORTS:

Los Angeles
Saturday, July 13, 1918

Continuing on the above entitled case I arose at 7:30 AM and proceeded to ascertain the owner of Car License No. 358838 and learned that it belonged to W. L. Haywood residing at the Melrose Hotel located at 120 South Grand Ave. This accomplished I boarded a car for Hollywood where I joined Investigator #140 and resumed surveillance of the residence in question.

We ascertained by telephone and visits to the apartment that no one was in or would come to the door, reporting same to Manager G.P.P. by telephone. No one entered or left said residence.

At 5:30 PM we phoned Manager G.P.P. and was instructed to discontinue and returned to the office as he had learned that the subject was in New York, whereupon we boarded a car for Los Angeles arriving there at 6:15 PM and after writing this report I discontinued at 6:30 PM.

EXPENSES:	Lunch	$ .50
	Carfare	$ .15
	Telephone calls	$ .10

TIME	One day	$8.00
		$8.75

Los Angeles
July 13, 1918

(Copy)
Mr. William Fox
New York City

My dear Mr. Fox:

I wish to acknowledge your telegram of July 12th as follows:

"I am informed Jewel Carmen is in New York — has she left the studio and if so wire me why she left to my home in Hewlett Bay Park Long Island."

In reply I wired you as follows: "Replying your telegram reference Jewel Carmen — when Carmen began her first picture with director Thornby after her first trip to New York after she had been on picture two weeks she produced a doctor's certificate that she was very ill and could only work two hours a day under the circumstances. I did my best to finish the picture at minimum cost — I knew this to be a stall and at conclusion of picture I told her unless she was willing to work at director's orders we would make no more pictures with her until she was in good health and she would not be paid any salary during such period — she agreed to work at our wishes and Thornby finished his second picture in fifteen days at cost of fourteen thousand dollars.

"Carmen came to see me at finish of second picture which was July sixth and said she was ready to start next picture immediately — the scenario for this picture is now ready and we begin erecting sets Monday — I heard rumours of Carmen having left city the early part of week and I immediately tried to verify them — I was unable to get any of her family and I could not get into communication with Carmen although I sent her two telegrams instructing her to call to see me also I have had Burns detectives on this matter past two days so far they have been unable to find out if she has left town or not — If Carmen has left Los Angeles she has no reason I know of for doing so except she wants us to fire her — have had nothing but trouble with her — and sending her today formal notice to report for work on Monday and if she does not report will stop her salary — if you decide to stop making pictures with Carmen can you send Peggy Hyland to take her place as I would like to keep director Thornby — he made first Carmen picture for twenty-three thousand under greatest difficulties and second picture for fourteen thousand — believe him to be a good asset for us — please advise writing in full today."

Supplementing my above telegram to you, I will state briefly my dealing with Carmen since her return from New York about ten weeks ago:

Soon after her return, or soon after she left Los Angeles, rumours came to my attention about stories that Carmen had been circulating stories of a most infamous kind about myself and my assistant Mr. Seiler. Of course, I paid no attention to them as it is a very common occurrence for such stories to get around in all Los Angeles studios. However, they became so persistent, and finally Tom Mix told me that these stories had been told to him by a chauffeur who had been taking Carmen to and from our studio. I called this chauffeur into my office and after questioning him he admitted that Carmen had told him many times that Mr. Seiler and I had made propositions to her. A few days later Carmen came back to Los Angeles; I called her into my office, confronted her with these statements, and had the chauffeur in my office at the same time. Carmen did not deny that she had made these statements, but I made her admit that at no time had Mr. Seiler or I treated her in anything but a courteous and gentlemanly way. I told her then if she would make any more statements of that kind I would have her arrested.

I then received your instructions to continue her in pictures, and although I am sure that if I had informed you then of the above facts you would never have featured her again, still I disregarded my personal feeling entirely in the matter, and did not write you.

I then engaged Thornby to direct her and began on her picture. After Thornby had been on the picture two weeks and had another week's work to finish the picture (and if the picture had been made without interruption it would have cost not more that $15,000 instead of $23,000) Carmen came to the studio one day about two o'clock with a doctor's certificate to the effect that she could not work more than two hours a day. I immediately had our studio doctor get in touch with her doctor and verify it. Carmen's doctor wrote our doctor a letter about her ailment (copy of this letter herewith enclosed). This letter has a lot of medical terms, which in plain English as our Dr. Ferry told me, meant that about four years ago Carmen suffered from a venereal disease and had an operation performed on her which had a tendency to leave her in a very nervous state, although previous to this I had never known or seen her to be nervous. In fact, when Lloyd and Franklin directed her she was able to work some days for twelve hours without ill effects. Although Carmen told me she was constantly under her doctor's care I found that she only went to him once for the purpose of getting the certificate and never went to him again. Under the circumstances and her refusing to work more than two hours a day Mr. Thornby and I tried to do our best to finish the picture the best we could, and where Thornby originally figured on making it three weeks it took him almost five weeks.

At the conclusion of this picture, I called her into my office and told her unless she was willing to work as we wanted her to, we would not make any more pictures with her until she was in good health, and during the period of her layoff would not pay her any salary. I was advised by our attorney, Mr. Wright, that we were within our rights to do this. Carmen said she thought she would be able to work as we wanted her to, and in order to make up for the first picture, Thornby made the second one in fifteen days at a cost of $14,000, working day and night to do it, and Carmen did not seem to feel any worse for it.

At the finish of the second picture we immediately began preparing a story, *The Man Catcher* which I wired Leo to buy and which he has since bought. The scenario for this story is almost finished and we are beginning to put up sets Monday. I saw Miss Carmen last Saturday, July 6th, on her return from location, and she told me she was ready to start the next picture immediately. She did not seem to have any grievances, and seemed to be feeling very good.

About three or four days after I had seen her, I heard rumours of her leaving for New York, and I immediately set out to verify them. I tried to get into telephone communication with her, but could not, neither could I get in touch with any of her family. I sent her two telegrams asking her to call to see me with reference to her next story, but got no reply. I then had the Burns Detective agency try to find out if she had left, and they could not get any information, so that I really had no means of knowing if she is in town or not; however, your telegram to me convinces me that she is in New York. I found that her last salary check which was given to her sister (At Carmen's request) on Tuesday July 9th was deposited in Carmen's bank, endorsed in her name, however, in her sister's handwriting.

I am writing her today to report ready for work on Monday, July 15th, and that if she does not report, her salary will be stopped.

I have consulted with our attorney Wright in the matter so that our legal position will be secure. Through Mr. Wright and other sources, I learned that Carmen's real name is Florence LaVina Quick, that she became notorious about four years ago in a certain action that involved some of the most prominent people of Los Angeles, and that she at that time was sentenced to a House of Correction. At that time she was an inmate of a notorious house in the city, known as the Jonquil House. During this trial she was examined by physicians, and they agreed that she was afflicted with a disease (I don't remember the medical term) where she is obsessed with the idea that every man she comes in contact with has or has tried to have intercourse with her. In fact, she brought a damage suit for $150,000 against a prominent automobile merchant in Los Angeles which was thrown out of court, and she also accused a well known judge of the city for the same thing, which charges were unfounded. Nearly all of the above was told to me by Mr. Wright and Mr. Wright said I could mention his name in writing to you.

It is my firm belief that Carmen should never again be featured in a picture by the Fox Film Corporation; it is also my opinion that she should never be allowed to get out of her contract, that she should be humiliated and belittled in every way so that her reputation, in so far as the screen is concerned, should be forever ruined, and teach her a lesson and through her teach others under contract a lesson. If we were to overlook her actions, it would demoralize our entire organization.

I will be frank to say to you that during the time she made her last two pictures, I have had many unhappy and miserable days, for during that time I had to humour and be pleasant and nice to an unprincipled, immoral and unmoral creature, whom you tried to raise out of the gutter, and her only thanks and appreciations have been to act in the way she has. However, there is one thing I would like you to do: if you decide not to let her out of her contract, and she reports back to our studios for work, I would like to handle her in the way she deserves to be handled.

In writing this letter, I may have at times used strong language, however, it comes from the heart, and is exactly how I feel, and I know you would want me to write the exact truth of the entire matter and my feeling as to the same.

Whether you decide that you want to keep director Thornby and send someone else for him to direct, or not, I would like you to feel that he deserves a great deal of credit, for at the time I engaged him he was employed and wanted to continue with his other concern, and I finally induced him to come with us and he, I think, did wonders in view of the trouble he had with Carmen, especially as it was his first picture for the company and he wanted to make a good showing. Any other director in a similar position, would I am sure have quit the picture without finishing it.

I presume, however, by the time you have received this letter, I will have had telegraphic instructions from you settling this entire situation; however, I feel that you should know the entire history of the matter.

> With kindest reads, I am,
> Respectfully yours,
> Sol M. Wurtzel

Even though Wurtzel admitted that his information about Jewel Carmen was hearsay, he did not hesitate to use it to justify his indignation against her for giving him such a bad time. Factually, what he recounted to Fox was a jumble of several notorious trials that had taken place in Los Angeles four years before his arrival.

In the spring of 1913, the city was rocked by the exposure of a "white slavery ring" and a subsequent Grand Jury investigation. The general public was made aware of the type of young women who tenanted the Jonquil Apartments on North Spring Street and of the prominent and wealthy men who patronized the adjoining "bath parlor."

The disclosures came about when three of the brazen young ladies, Cleo Helen Barker, Irene Brown-Levy and Jeanette Ellis, accused a Long Beach multi-millionaire of "maliciously assaulting, wounding and bruising" them and sued him for a total of $150,000. In the past, when various patrons had been so threatened, the men paid up so that the girls would shut up. Mrs. Jose Rosenberg, the proprietess, would accept the money on her abused girls' behalf after her personal lawyer made the gentlemen aware of the delinquencies to which they were contributing. But finally the successful technique met a hitch. G.H. Bixby refused to be blackmailed. He was acquitted after a lengthy trial and his defense, handled by the town's leading attorneys, was reputed to have cost him $50,000.

Running concurrently with the Bixby trial were those of Richard Hollingsworth and William LaCasse. These two young men-about-town were charged with contributing to the delinquency of Evelyn Quick who described herself as a motion picture actress — an occupational designation used by many young women to get around the city's strict vagrancy laws.

Hollingsworth was not a "prominent automobile merchant" as described by Wurtzel but a car salesman and although Alice Quick, a sister of the complaining witness, gave testimony at a closed hearing no public mention was made of any Florence LaVina Quick. However, several of the women who had figured in the grand jury investigation and Bixby trial were called upon to appear as witnesses in the case.

The judge declared that Hollingsworth and LaCasse would have to stand trial in Superior Court and fixed their bail at $1,000. Two months later their cases came to trial. The District Attorney admitted there were contradictions in the testimony of Miss Quick, her mother and sisters, and the two men testified that the evening in question had been spent in good clean fun at the LaCasse bungalow. The young people had danced and played the piano and the girls went home early. The all male jury failed to reach a verdict and the case was dismissed.

Whether Jewel Carmen was unjustly maligned or not, the Fox Film Corporation soon dispensed with her services. Then, it was business as usual at Western Ave.

New York City
August 19, 1918

Mr. Sol M. Wurtzel
Los Angeles

My dear Sol:

I wish to acknowledge receipt of your letter of August 10th. I have sent you the following wire: "*Girl I Left Behind Me* play that dealt with Indian trouble. In my opinion that is thing of the past today. Therefore not interested in making this film at present time — Bessie Barriscale* at

Popular leading lady.

present in Los Angeles and unemployed. Find out if available and what price — Our desire is to use her in Excel Program."

After I have read *The Road to Berlin*, I will write to you my opinion of it. You already know my opinion on doing *The Girl I Left Behind Me* at the present time. This would be a serious mistake. This play deals with the Indian question. I talked to Farnum and Lloyd about the same long before we were not in this war as deep as we are now. With the present war conditions I do not think the public is interested in our previous Indian troubles. For that reason this story is rejected for the present and I urge that you immediately search for a vehicle to take its place. In addition to this the Charles Frohman Estate would be entitled to 1 percent of the gross on *The Girl I Left Behind Me*, if we made a new version of it. In addition to this vehicle being made, the author's royalties would be greater than that which we are willing to contract for now with an author for a brand-new play. However, my opinion at this time is not based on the royalty question but rather on the fact that I do not think this story is a proper one to make at this time.

I again wish to remind you that you have a wonderful vehicle entitled *Pierre Legrande.* I expect to remind you of this every time you are about to start a vehicle. I do not mind doing this because it required the same urging before I could get Lewis* to see *The Bondsmand* or Lloyd to see *Les Miserables* and if they do not adopt *Pierre Le Grande* as a story at this time, they will in the near future.[†]

With reference to the paragraph on *By Right of Conquest*, I have heard so much about this that there is no need of writing any further. My understanding is now that you will not do this story.

I am not interested in Mae Murray nor in her director.

I have read your letter with reference to Bara and I am now thoroughly conversant with the facts as you describe them.

Upon receipt of this letter you will arrange for an increase in your salary of $50 per week.

In going over the weekly payroll vouchers I notice you are paying your assistant $90 per week at this time. I am sorry that you saw fit to give your assistant two advances without first consulting me. You know that one of the grave objections that I had to Carlos was that he felt he had reached the stage where he no longer needed to consult with me. You, however, definitely understood that you at no time would reach the stage where you were not to communicate with me before taking any definite action. Your assistant's salary when he started in Los Angeles was $2,600 per year, which is greater than what he earned during all the years

*Edgar Lewis — director. †It was never made.

that he was a school teacher. Without my knowledge and consent you advanced his salary in February to $3800 a year, and without further consent on my part in July to $4600 a year. I cannot quite understand the reason for all this without first writing to me and getting my consent. If perchance, you have reached the stage where you imagine that you need no longer consult with me, let this communication then be notice on you that I expect you to consult with me on all matters out of the usual routine, and that you are to take no action without first consulting with me and first receiving my consent.

At the present time the only employee bonded at Los Angeles is R.E. Olin.* I ask you to send me a list of those employees who are handling cash for the company and name the amount that you think the company should bond these employees for.

I write to inquire in what condition is the matter of Davis and the other employees who you said stole film. What has the bonding company done in connection therewith? You have failed to make a report in this matter since its occurrence.

Are you acquainted with the fact that Waldo (Edward) is to be assigned to the studios and is it your idea to have him replace Olin or will you require the services of both? We have replaced Waldo in New York with Mr. O'Donohue, and Waldo will be ready to leave for Los Angeles within the next four or five weeks.

> With kindest regards, I am
> Very truly yours,
> (signed) William Fox

> Los Angeles
> August 26, 1918

Mr. William Fox (Personal)
New York City

Dear Mr. Fox:

I wish to acknowledge your letter of August 19th, and I will answer all the paragraphs in rotation.

Regarding *The Girl I Have Left Behind Me*, on receipt of your telegram of August 19th, I took the matter up with Lloyd and explained your views to him. Since then, the story *Freedom* by E. Lloyd Sheldon has been purchased. Lloyd and Farnum will do this as their next and then do *The Last of the Duanes* by Zane Grey. Inasmuch as *The Road to Berlin* deals with the war and Freedom also touches on the war, I doubt very much whether Farnum will do the former story; I am therefore trying to

*Company Auditor

sell *The Road to Berlin* to some other producing company so that we will not be out the money that was paid for it.

I have not forgotten *Pierre Legrand* and I have been urging it on Lloyd time and again, and I will continue to do so. At this time, it is a question in my mind whether Lloyd will do another, or more than another picture with Farnum due to the draft; Lloyd has been receiving with Farnum due to the draft; Lloyd has been receiving notices from the British Commission to enlist and so far has not made up his mind what to do. Should he enlist I will wire you in due time so that arrangements can be made in plenty of time to get another director for Farnum.

I note your kindness in increasing my salary $50.00 per week beginning with today, for which I wish to sincerely thank you.

I note your paragraph with reference to my increasing the salary of my assistant to $90.00 per week without first consulting with you. The reason I did not first notify you was because I considered it the usual routine of business here as during the past ten months the salaries of nearly all the older employees have been increased. I increased his salary for two reasons; first, his work has been very satisfactory and valuable in every way; he is doing the work that formerly three men did, whose combined salaries were twice that which he is now getting; second he is class 3A in the draft, although unmarried, due to the fact that his parents are dependent upon him and he sends them one-third of his salary every week. If it were not for the latter, he would now be in the army and I would have to get another assistant, and it would be pretty difficult matter to get a capable assistant and a man whom I could trust out here. In the future, I will allow no increases in salary to anyone unless they first have your approval.

I wish to call to your attention, however, that beginning with Wednesday, August 28th, there will be an increase in the wages of the following employees:

Electricians	From	$5.00 to $6.00 per day
Carpenters	"	$5.00 to $6.00 per day
Propertymen	"	$30.00 to $35.00 weekly
Ass't	"	$4.00 to $5.00 per day

also double time for Work on Sundays, July 4th, Thanksgiving Day, Christmas and New Year's Day; also time and one-half for overtime on week days.

These increases were demanded by the theatrical and studio employees of Los Angeles through their union, known as the Theatrical Stage Employees Alliance, and at a meeting of the various studio managements held Saturday, August 24th, at which were present Lasky, Fox, Universal, Triangle, Pathe, Vitagraph, Metro, Sennett, Griffith, and others, it was decided to have each studio treat with their men individually and allow the increases or not as each studio saw fit; however, not to treat with the union and ignore them entirely. At some of the studios the new wage scale had already been in existence; the others decided to give increases only where necessary and if the men were deserving of it. In our studio, I am increasing the wages of those men who have been regularly employed since January 1st, 1918, and to the rest pay the old wage. I do not know at this writing if this will be satisfactory as they may insist on all the men getting the new wage increase. I will keep you advised fully in the matter. One thing, all the studio managements decided on was that all studios be conducted on the "open shop" policy. I am enclosing herewith the notices sent to the various studious by the Theatrical Stage Employee Alliance.

Replying to the paragraph 4, page 2 of your letter, at no time have I felt the stage where I imagine I need no longer consult with you, nor do I ever expect to reach that stage; if I ever feel that I have reached that stage, I will be the first to advise you.

I wish to call the following to your attention; the salary of Lynn Reynolds, director for Tom Mix, has been $400.00 weekly since he began work on *The Two Gun Man*, and after he completes *The Two Gun Man* and two other pictures his salary will be $450.00. I made this arrangement after he had completed *Mr. Logan, U.S.A.*, due to the fact that he asked for an increase then, as he had received outside offers far in excess of what we were then paying him. Also, the salary of director E.J. LeSaint, beginning with his present picture, on August 19th, was increased to $400 for the same reason. The salary of LeSaint's cameraman, Baker, has been increased from $100 to $125 weekly. Baker has been with us ever since LeSaint came and had not received in increase before. However, as I said before, no increases of salary to anyone will be made without first getting your approval.

At the present time, the following employees in the Los Angeles studios are bonded:

R.E. Olin, auditor	for $5,000
J.J. Lane, cashier	for $5,000
Robtr. Greene, timekeeper	for $1,000

The only other employees who handle cash are the assistant directors, and they only handle small amounts from $25 to $100; when a company goes away on location and need large sums of money, it is turned over to the director himself, who is responsible for it.

Regarding the matter of Davies and the stolen film, I enclose herewith copies of correspondence that passed between us on March 8th, 9th and 19th. The Horsleys were not prosecuted, and Davies pleaded guilty but was given a suspended sentence.

I have not been acquainted with the fact that Waldo is to be assigned

to the Los Angeles studios. I do not know now whether to replace him
with Olin, as Olin has done excellent work and has been here for quite
some time; it is probable however, that by the time Waldo gets here other
employees in the department of draft age will have been called, and
Waldo can take their places and work in conjunction with Olin. During
the past six months we have lost about 25 percent of our best men
through the draft.

My brother, Sam, about whom you wired me on August 20th has
been drafted, and leaves for Tucson, Arizona on September 1st. My
mother, who I wired you on August 21st was on the point of death, died
Sunday August 24th.

At this time, Reynolds has finished photographing the *Two Gun-
Man*, and is on his way back from Prescott, Ariz. where the entire picture
was photographed, but from what I have seen, I have no doubt but what
it will be as good or better than the previous Mix pictures. His next picture will be *The Coming of the Law*. I received your letter regarding Mix,
and on his return will take the matter up with him and advise you.

LeSaint began photographing today on *Love's Pilgrimage*, copy of
scenario has already been sent you. He will finish this in about three
weeks, and will then do *Quicksands* which Leo purchased in New York.

Edwards finishes his present picture about September 13th, Miss
Bara will leave for New York on September 15th and Edwards will leave
on the 20th. The picture *The She Devil* is now being cut, and I hope to be
able to ship it by September 1st.

> With kindest regards, I am
> Respectfully yours,
> Sol M. Wurtzel

*None of the correspondence remains from the following ten months; the col-
lection resumes with a voluminous letter from Fox written in June of 1919, after
his first post-war trip to Europe. In it, he reviews with unsurpassable sarcasm
and scorn his protégé's output of films for the year past.*

*William Fox divided his employees into two categories and treated them in a
diverse manner. With his important stars, directors and foreign managers, his
behavior was impeccable, even to the point of generosity if required. He would
save his spleen to vent unrestrainedly on his immediate working family of
employees; those with whom he had continuing direct contact. He was the pro-
totype of the tyrannical father who would keep his children obedient by berat-
ing and humiliating them.*

*Wurtzel replied with an equally lengthy letter in which he humbly and care-
fully covered every point brought up by his boss. Detail after detail was enu-
merated and documented, resulting in a comprehensive description of motion
picture production in Los Angeles following World War I.*

New York City
June 23, 1919

Mr. Sol M. Wurtzel
Los Angeles

My dear Sol:

Since I have returned from Europe, I have reviewed the following comedies:

Her First Kiss
His Naughty Wife
Dabbling In Society

I consider these excellent comedies.

In addition thereto, I have reviewed the comedy *Footlight Maids.* This I consider impractical, impossible and unreleasable, and I have ordered it thrown into the waste heap, regardless of the opinion of those you have surrounding you in Los Angeles, who might have told you that the picture is possible.

I have also reviewed the Tom Mix pictures: *Wilderness Trail* and *Romance of Cow Hollow.* Both of these I consider fine pictures.

I have likewise reviewed the Tom Mix picture *High Speed*, which I consider impossible for release without destroying all the good work that we have accomplished with Mix. This picture is excellent in the first reel and is excellent in the last reel. The three center reels are long, dragged out, drawn out, unexciting, and cannot be released in its present form. At this time, I am not prepared to send it back with recommendations as to how to remedy it, but will do so in the near future. I question the wisdom of returning it to have it re-arranged. I did that already with two different subjects, one the Tom Mix picture *Coming of the Law*, and the other the Brockwell picture called *Gypsy Love*. When I reviewed these pictures, after you were supposed to have corrected them, I was unable to find any scenes contained in the original pictures. In fact, the cost of remaking them was as great as the original cost of the making of the pictures. Therefore, the only thing that happened was the original pictures were practically destroyed and new pictures were made; in fact, it would have been better so, because then a brand new story could have been rewritten and made, rather than to be obliged to stick to the original story, which was impossible, and necessitated the returning of the film for remaking. This is particularly so in the Brockwell subject, where I failed to find a single foot of the original story. I have asked Leo to advise you to return this picture, which I understand you have already done.

Please explain the reason for the necessity of such drastic steps as were taken with these two pictures, and why you did not first communicate with me telling me that the other pictures were of no value, and that you would be obliged to make them all over again.

At the time of this writing, I have also had projected for me the first two reels of the Brockwell picture called *Sadie*. I do no know what the other three reels contain. I expect to look at those after this letter has left in the mail, but from what I have seen in the first two reels, the story is impossible. You have permitted them to develop the first two reels of the story of *Sadie* and make of it a comedy. You must well know that Miss Brockwell is not a comedian, and that the Fox Film Corporation has no desire to make comedy pictures with her. When I review the other three reels of this story, I will advise you further as to what my opinion of this picture is, and whether it is possible to release. From what I have seen in the first two reels, it is fit for the junk pile. I have also reviewed the three pictures by *Millarde* (Harry) with *Traverse.** I consider these three pictures excellent ones.

I have reviewed the two pictures made by *Edwards* with *Farnum*. I consider these two pictures excellent pictures.

There is now ready for me to see a picture with Peggy Hyland. I will write to you after I have reviewed it.

I am fully aware that it is hardly possible to make all pictures 100 percent, but there seems to be no excuse for the miserable picture originally made of *Gypsy Love* which was ruined by being miscast, or for the making of *Sadie*, which as I said before, I have not seen in its entirety, but from its first two reels it is very evident that the picture does not contain a Brockwell story, and may likewise necessitate being discarded. If I failed to tell you before, take this for notice that I do not want any pictures made with Brockwell, unless they are intense, dramatic stories. If there is to be any comedy in the picture at all, it is to be incidental to the story.

While on the subject of the two pictures which were returned to you to be remade, I wish to call to your attention that *The Sneak* (*Gypsy Love*) cost $41,600, which is twice as great as *Divorce Trap*, *Scarlet Road* and *Moral Law*, all by far better pictures than *The Sneak*.

Coming of the Law, as a result of making two pictures and only having one, cost $61,500, which is twice as great as *Six Shooter Andy*, *Western Blood*, *Ace High*, *Fame and Fortune*, *Hell Roarin' Reform*, all very excellent, splendid, spectacular productions.

I presume by the time you receive this letter, that Walsh has left Los Angeles with the picture *Evangeline*. Whether this is a good or a bad picture, you will not be blamed for it, as I fully realize that you have had little or no control over his actions.

*Madeline Traverse — leading lady.

I understand that there is now in transit three more comedies. I am in hopes that they will be of a character which will be of credit to the Fox Film Corporation.

In the comedy, *His Naughty Wife*, you will recall there was a lengthy episode devoted to five or six small children. This episode will be an acceptable one to the public, and I urge that in future comedies, many episodes with small babies and children be inserted, for there is nothing more pleasing to the eye, and nothing that causes greater laughter than does a children interest.

When I returned from Europe, I was mortified to find the great quantity of money that Leo is wiring you each week, and naturally, I sat down to analyze, to find out why this amount was necessary, and why in spite of these large sums wired each week, you still have an indebtedness owing to merchants of approximately *$70,000*. Of course, $50,000 of this outstanding is the waste occasioned by the remaking of the *Coming of the Law* and *The Sneak*, but still does not account for the great tremendous sums which are wired to you each Saturday. My analysis shows me that the cause for these extraordinary amounts which you require each Saturday, is as follows:

1st. Last year we engaged a director by the name of Gillstrom (Arvid E.), who made two pictures in New York with Jane and Catherine Lee,* one costing $19,000 and the other costing $16,000. Both of these were accepted by the public as splendid pictures. Gillstrom asked to be sent to California, because he said that these two pictures cost too much money, caused by the lack of facilities here in New York; that if he was permitted to work on the Fox Film lot in Los Angeles, with the facilities there, he could make the pictures for at least 25 percent less. As a result of his going to California, he made a picture called *Smiles*, the cost of which was $34,300, or as much as both of the other pictures together.

My correspondence to you last year, gave you the amount to be expended on Hyland and Traverse pictures, which were pictures sold in the Excel Brand. In spite of that, I find that the Hyland picture released on March 23rd, which was after my departure for abroad, called *The Rebellious Bride*, cost $28,000 — the following picture called *Miss Adventure* cost $36,500, and another picture that we have here called *Cowardice Court*, not released as yet, $33,800.

None of the last mentioned three pictures were of any especial value. They were stupid, insipid pictures, and I call your attention, in comparison to the cost of the four *Millarde* pictures made with *Traverse*, each one being an excellent, pretentious production, well-staged and mounted, and pictures which will help to make Traverse popular.

*Sister child-stars who were featured in many Fox productions.

The Love That Dares — one of the finest pictures we have had this year — cost $23,000.

Gambling in Souls—$26,000

When Fate Decides—$24,000

Until Eternity—$26,700

While it is true that even these four pictures cost an average of $5,000 more than we originally planned, I will state below the reason why they had this increased cost. However, something must have gone wrong with the Hyland pictures, considering the comparison in the cost of the Traverse pictures as against the cost of the Hyland pictures. My analysis is as follows:

1st . That the sets used for the pictures in this brand of film are all too large and stupendous, with too much furniture in them. The size of the sets is caused by the fact that you have so much stage room. That the director's ambition is to find just how large he can possibly build them, and instead of these sets helping the picture, they detract from the dramatic value, and cause the cost of the picture to go up.

2nd. You know that we have no desire to have Hyland or Traverse pictures released on the Excel Brand in more than 4,200 feet, titles and all. None of the pictures that you are sending in are below the 5,000 feet mark. Therefore, one-fifth too many scenes are being photographed, and this one-fifth is what is causing the increased cost, plus the extravagant mounting and size of sets that you are building.

It is hardly believable, when one analyzes the cost of the Tom Mix pictures, which are large and spectacular, with many people, many horses and many other things that cause the cost to go up, that in spite of all that, it is possible to make these pictures for considerable less money than you have permitted to be expended for Peggy Hyland pictures. I have already quoted to you the cost of the Mix pictures. Compare them with the cost of the three Hyland pictures referred to.

I call your particular attention to the fact that the last Hyland picture, which just came in and which I have not as yet reviewed, but made by Lawrence* whom we have sent to you from New York, cost up to the week ending June 7th, according to your cost sheet, $22,592. This, of course, is $10,000 cheaper than the three pictures I have pointed out above, but is still too great, because Lawrence, who has worked, as you know, in the East for a year and a half, has never made a picture with Pearson, with all the lack of facilities that we have and with Pearson's salary double that of Hyland, which cost more than $20,000, and many of them costing inside of $18,000. Which is the object of making pictures in California, when in New York, we

*Edmund Lawrence — director.

have a director who makes stupendous pictures of intense, dramatic value, with an artist like Pearson requiring well-mounted productions, great supporting cast, plenty of preparation, and still finish the production at a cost of $18,000? What is the use of going to California with the same director directing Miss Hyland, with the cost of his picture already reported as of June 7th at $22,592, and probably a great portion more to be added to it? Is it not evident to you that there is something radically wrong?

The three outstanding features that are wrong are as follows:

1st: That the pictures made for the Excel program are 20 percent too long, as quoted above.

2nd: That the sets are entirely too large.

3rd: One of the most important things that we find in examining your payrolls, is that the man who is engaging your talent in the supporting casts is expending sums of money never heard of here in the East. In examining the Hyland cast, we find that you are paying as high as $300 for a girl to play opposite Hyland and $250 for a man to play opposite Hyland. We can readily understand the necessity for paying a fair price, if leading men are scarce, to get one who will help the picture, but by no possible method of calculation, can we possibly figure out how in God's world, you can hire a girl to support Miss Hyland and pay her $300 when in New York no one was ever hired to play in a picture with her who ever received more than a $100 salary. The supporting casts in the *Traverse, Hyland and Brockwell* pictures are all high, and this is particularly evident, when Mr. Edwards' cast is examined, and we find that of twenty performers in a company, he has fifteen of them whose salaries do not average over $75 a week.

4th: Another reason for the high cost of your pictures is the expensive rental prices paid for the hiring of furniture and props, and the tremendous overhead which you suffer; also the cost of the great list of automobiles which you have, plus the automobile hire that you have each week in spite of the many automobiles that we now own.

So much for the Excel Brand.

The Victory Brand of pictures in which Tom Mix and Gladys Brockwell appear — it is perfectly agreeable to the Fox Film Corp. to make wonderful, splendid productions as we have made in the past with Tom Mix, excluding the last one which you just sent in, for the present cost, if all of the money is carefully and judiciously expended, for it is our ambition to make better and finer pictures with Mix each time, inasmuch as we are especially interested in him due to the fact that we have a possibility of reselling these pictures to the exhibitors and renting them at a fair price, which will warrant the expenditure.

I am not attempting to analyze the cost of the Farnum pictures, for I know that Mr. Edwards does not spend a single penny more than he has

to, for he, as you know, has my explicit faith and confidence. When replying to this letter, please do not refer to any automobile hire necessary for
Mr. Edwards, Mr. Farnum, or his company, for I am not now finding fault
with the cost of any of the pictures made by Mr. J. Gordon Edwards.

Referring again to the high cost of your productions in the Excel
Brand, I wish to state the following:

Because of the fact that the sets used for this brand of film are so
large, it is only natural that it should be necessary for you to engage a 25
percent larger number of carpenters, a 25 percent larger number of electricians, a 25 percent larger number of property men and all other help
necessary to handle, and build these tremendous sets which you are now
building. For the pictures made in the Excel Brand, there can possibly be
no harm in using many of the same interiors in two or three pictures, so
long as they are furnished slightly different and that the camera shoots
these sets at a slightly different angle.

I fully realize that a great part of this is probably my own fault,
because of the fact that I have over-burdened you with work, and probably the job has gotten beyond you; for when I look around me in the
East, I find that of all the pictures we are making, we have only two companies working here. This, of course, will be changed materially shortly,
Walsh having already left; I presume Edwards will come East soon, and
we have engaged other stars here with whom we expect to make pictures
in the East. In fact, when Fall comes, and our new plant opens here, at
least 50 percent or more of the pictures will be made in New York.

Because of the few companies that we have here now, we find that
we can readily give Mr. Samuel F. Kingston* a rest and a vacation, and I
have requested him to spend his vacation in Los Angeles, where he may
be of material help to you —first, in engaging artists for the supporting
casts, and second, in such other capacities as you will devise between you
in which he can make himself generally useful.

It is hardly fair for me to expect you to be able to practice economy,
and properly supervise all of the work occasioned by the great number of
companies that you have in Los Angeles these past three months, and it is
because of this fact, that I felt you should be relieved of a portion of your
work for at least two months, which will be the length of Mr. Kingston's
stay in California. He comes to you extending the hand of a friend, with
instructions from me to be of every possible aid to you. You, in return, are
expected to extend him every possible courtesy and to permit him to be of
real, material help while in California, so that when he returns to the East,
he may be in a position to say only complimentary things about you.

Manager — New York Studio

The Board of Directors of the Fox Film Corporation held a meeting a week ago, and inquired into the necessity of sending to Los Angeles the great quantity of money each week, and the necessity for the liability that we have in Los Angeles. During that conference, they learned of the fact that money is wired in the name of the Wm. Fox Vaud. Co. and withdrawn from the bank on checks signed by you. I was severely criticized for permitting that, for they called to my attention that same was contrary to the By-Laws of the Corporation, and particularly called my attention to the fact that here in New York, where money is being expended under our very nose, that no checks leave New York without being signed by myself and Mr. Leo, or myself and Mr. Eisele* or by Mr. Eisele and Mr. Leo, and that if there is a necessity for two signatures in New York, there surely should not have been a variation from that policy in connection with the money expended in Los Angeles, and it is because of this that Mr. Samuel Kingston is bringing with him a set of bank resolutions, authorizing the bank to make no further payments of money belonging to the Wm. Fox Vaudeville Co. or the Fox Film Corporation unless the checks are signed by you and counter-signed by Kingston. You will understand, that this is no reflection on you; that the method now being adopted is similar to that which, as you know, has always been in practice here in New York, and which foolishly I never have adopted in Los Angeles, and which is now necessary, as protection for yourself, because of the great sum of money which is being expended, the total of which for this current year will amount to in excess of two million dollars.

The auditors who have examined the books of the Fox Film Corporation, find that we have lost money on that brand of pictures known as the Excel Brand, because of the fact that we are unable to sell them in the United States for more than $40,000 per picture. For these $40,000, we are obliged to supply the rights of the negative, the great quantity of positive required, the cost of overhead, and the combined cost of all this is many thousands of dollars per picture in excess of our revenue. It is probably this, more than anything else, which is causing me to write to you at this great length, to bring to your attention the absolute necessity of reducing the cost of this brand of pictures, so that we may be able to sell them and continue to earn a profit, of if, after you have employed the economics described above, to wit:

1st: Reducing the size of the sets.

2nd: Reducing the cost of the supporting cast.

3rd: Reducing the length of the pictures.

4th: Because of the last three, reducing the number of help required to do all of the above—

*John Eisele — the Corporation Treasurer.

if, in spite of all this, the cost cannot be brought down so that the Fox Film Corp. can make a profit, it will be better off to know it at the earliest possible moment, and discontinue making a brand of film on which it is obliged to lose money.

It has been a considerable time since you have left New York. I am, of course, assuming that you are the same man who left my office before you went to California; that your manners and *habits* have not changed any, and I am writing this letter as though you were sitting in front of me and I were talking to you, based on your mental capacity when you used to sit before me and take my dictation.

If you have changed in any manner, will you please specifically describe in what way, and what caused any change in you since you left here. All of the above is written to you in a spirit of friendship and affection, for in spite of the tremendous costs of many of the pictures, and in spite of the many extravagances, and in spite of everything that I may have said above, you are still to be congratulated upon having risen to the size and heights to be able to have conducted my business in the manner that you have, and the fault is to be found with me in piling too much work on you, and not sending someone from New York long before this to share the responsibility with you.

If, upon the receipt of this note, you find that in addition to Kingston, it would be of help to you to have Bach* there (if you are afraid that that department has gotten away from you and you feel that you ought to be re-entrenched with Bach for two months to supervise the construction of sets, etc.) wire, and I will send him on to Los Angeles.

Jack Leo showed me a letter where you have loaned Tom Mix $2,500. It is indeed a pleasure to me to serve Tom Mix† in extending to him this loan. Tell Tom that if he requires any further money, not to be backward, but to communicate with me direct, for I will be glad to loan him any sum that he may require.

I am inquiring, however, of you by what authority you had to make this loan without first communicating with me or with Mr. Jack Leo, so that we could have had this loan approved by our Executive Committee, and then have it properly submitted to our Board of Directors. Your attitude in this matter assumes a proportion far beyond anything that Carlos dared do during his regime.

I call to your attention that when you first came to me, your salary per year was less than one thousand dollars. I have permitted you to grow to your heights. On what theory did you take it upon yourself to loan money

---

*William Bach — *stage and set construction manager.* †Mix's salary at this time was $600 per week.*

belonging to the Company (which no one has a right to loan without it being approved by the Board of Directors under the Corporation Law of the State of New York) without first having received the approval therefor. I would like your complete explanation of this action, and the necessity for it, for I understand from Leo's letter, that you have already advanced this money and there was no strike on the Western Union or the Postal Telegraph, which would have made it impossible for you to have received our sanction.

Millarde returned, and while he reports that he did not seem to get along with you there while on the first picture, which I understand was during the time that Sheehan was there (which Sheehan reported to me was Millarde's fault and not yours— Sheehan reports that you called Millarde in your office and gave him a complete and definite understanding of what you expected him to do, for which I give you credit) that since then he and you have been good friends. He praises you highly as well as your administration, and says that no director has any possible alibi for any delay, as you are on the job all of the time watching everything that is going on, and that any director who has an alibi is lying and is stalling rather than being delayed because you do not extend to him every facility. I was indeed happy to receive his report.

If Millarde's report is correct, and if it does not come to me based on the assumption that some day he is going back to California, and he hopes to have you be more lenient with him, then my contention of the excess cost of pictures can only be because of the items described in this letter heretofore, and not because of your inability to properly handle the project, but rather that in your anxiety to build stupendous productions for a program that does not require them, the cost of these productions is too great.

Kingston is anxiously looking forward, on arriving in Los Angeles, to be of real, material help to you and to the corporation, and I look forward to a very clear, precise and mutual understanding between you, one that will result in a great benefit to the Fox Film Corporation.

In replying to this letter, I shall expect you to do so at great length, answering it paragraph per paragraph, confessing to those statements contained in my letter which are correct, and showing me if I am in error, in what items I am in error.

Also, advise me whether you have sufficient material for your directors, and whether your supply of stories is of a quantity to keep you going.

I have learned from Leo that on the cost sheet of the present Tom Mix picture, there appears no charge for a director, and that the chart is marked "Directed by Tom Mix." How did you reach the conclusion to let Tom direct himself? Is it because LeSaint fell down in this last picture which I have written on above, and is it because Tom Mix claimed that *Romance of Cow Hollow* had been directed by him rather than by the man whose name appears on the screen as director? Every once in a while, an artist could make a picture, probably without a director, but that would be bad policy as a general rule.

It is really surprising to me to see the excellent picture in *The Wilderness Trail*, and this poor picture — the last one you sent in. However, from the scenario, it is evident that this last picture could not possibly have been good, for it must have appeared in the scenario that after the first episode, or after the time that Tom went to California, that you cannot build a story upon a prize fight for three long reels; so that I rather find fault with you in permitting LeSaint to have ever started the story, for I have previously written to you that it is our desire to make pictures with Mix which will appeal to the women, and no one knows better than you, being a fighting fan, as I understand it, that women do not attend prize fights, and are not interested in motion pictures that are based on a prize fight. Therefore, I urge, as I said before that you make a complete search and find a real, wonderful, competent director, regardless of salary, who can make real wonderful pictures with Tom Mix stories, and if you find one, advise us so that we may negotiate for the purchase of it, for it seems to me that the main and principal thing is to have the foundation of a real story, and that is best developed from either a serial story running in a magazine, or from a book that contains a story which might have Tom Mix material. Although Leo tells me that *High Speed* was a book and that is was originally read in Los Angeles and you requested that we buy it, still I cannot possibly believe that you have ever read *High Speed* when you asked that it be purchased, for it must have been evident to you that the great and important thing in *High Speed* was the prize fight. The love interest in *High Speed* seems to be dragged in at the tail. It is the least part of the story; the story is complete without ever having introduced the little girl; she means nothing to the story at all, and all of this must have been evident if you had watched the takes when it was being photographed, and it was surely evident when the picture was completed, and never should have been sent here in its present condition.

I feel now that I have given you as much praise and criticism as on is entitled to in one day. Therefore, I will bring my letter to a close.

Trusting that this will reach you in good health, and looking forward to receiving from you an intelligent report, one that will be based on the future success of the Fox Film Corporation and yourself, and with kindest regards, I am, as ever,

Very truly yours,
(signed) William Fox

P.S. At first I intended to mail this letter and have it arrive in Los Angeles before Kingston did. On second thought, and to be sure that you will have it on his arrival, and to be sure that this letter does not fall into the hands of anyone else in the employ of the Company, I have given Kingston this letter to hand to you. I have requested that he hand it to you with the following statement: That you read it at your leisure, after you have welcomed him to Los Angeles, and that he sees you several hours after you have read the contents of this letter.

Dictated after the entire letter had been written:

Last year, you wrote to me and said that one of the reasons that the cost of the pictures was so high was due to the fact that we only had four directors working at the coast; that you were obliged to charge the overhead and divide it amongst these four directors, which caused each picture to cost several thousands of dollars more than they should ordinarily. You urged that I send you additional directors and additional companies. During the period of my complaint about the tremendous sums that we were obliged to wire you, you know that we have given you additional directors, for you have had during this period at least ten companies working, amongst which to divide the overhead. Still this division has not reduced the cost of the pictures, but has rather increased the cost.

I have reviewed the Hyland picture made by Lawrence,* and consider it a good picture, although nothing exceptional. I can now intelligently discuss with you the salary list in connection with that production.

Miss Hyland's salary, of course is as per contract, Hillarde's† salary at $200, you must know is more than he ever got here in the East. The woman who plays opposite Miss Hyland, to whom you paid $300 a week, I would not pay $10 a day to. She is a woman of great big size, unattractive, had an unimportant part which anyone would have played, and the person who played it should have hired by the day, and should not have received more than $10 a day. For the other members of the cast, the butler, the old man and the father, not one of these three characters would be entitled to more than $100 a week. Of course, if you are going to pay fancy salaries, as you have in the Hyland picture for the cast I have just seen on the screen, I can readily understand the tremendous cost of this production.

Also dictated after the entire letter had been written:

I have asked Mr. Kingston to discuss with you an article which appeared in the magazine of the Sunday World. I have instructed him to tell you just what attitude you are to take in the matter, and that without

---

*Edmund Lawrence — director. †Harry S. Hillarde-actor.

further conversation Marc Robbins* is to be dismissed, without being told why he is being dismissed or without discussing the proposition with him or with anyone else.

I have reviewed the comedy called *The Yellow Dog Catcher*, and consider it an excellent comedy.

Los Angeles
July 16, 1919

(Copy)
Mr. William Fox
New York City

My dear Mr. Fox:

Sam Kingston arrived in Los Angeles on June 30th. I met him at the station and welcomed him. He gave me your letter of June 23rd which I read in accordance with your instruction. After reading same I gave instructions to the employees of the studio that Mr. Kingston's orders were to be obeyed the same as if you or I would be giving them. I told Kingston that he had my heartiest co-operation in everything relating to the studio, and I am pleased to state that we have been getting along splendidly.

In accordance with your request that I send you an intelligent report on which will be based the future success of the Fox Film Corporation and on myself and to the statements contained in your letter with regards to the pictures and to other matters, I have hesitated answering your letter until today, so that I could read it over very carefully many times, investigate the statements contained therein in every detail and write you an intelligent and comprehensive reply.

I was pleased that you like the comedies *Her First Kiss*, *His Naughty Wife*, *Dabbling in Society* and *Yellow Dog Catcher*, and I hope you will like the comedies *Wild Waves and Women* and *Chicken a la Cabaret*, which by this time have no doubt reached you, equally as well or better. We now have in work four comedies which I hope to be able to ship by the end of this month and which I look forward to being very good, and I am also in hopes that the future comedies we make will improve in quality and be of lower cost. It is my wish that the comedies being made under the new organization be of such quality and low cost as to enable you to make up for the losses on all previous comedies made, and I am devoting to the comedies every possible moment of my time.

Regarding the comedy *Footlight Maids*, it is my great regret that this

*Head of the Los Angeles Story Dept.

comedy did not meet with your approval. However, I hope to profit by seeing that the future comedies that are made do not contain the elements that were objectionable to you.

In all our comedies we will endeavor to inject such material that the public will like in the way of children and babies, and especially such material as will be of interest to children, as you suggest.

In connection with the comedies I wish to state that when the new organization was started five months ago, our equipment necessary to make comedies was practically nil. All we had were some flats and the cyclorama. It has, therefore, been necessary for us to build an equipment which would enable us to make the comedies of the quality we required and in much quicker time than heretofore, and this equipment has amounted to a large sum of money. Very little of this is reflected in the cost of the comedies made now, but it will in the future. It has been necessary for us to build a sky backing which will cost approximately $3,000. This is of vital necessity in order to do certain trick stuff, the same as we use the cyclorama, and which will be the means of enabling us to save large sums of money in the comedies made in the future, for then our comedy companies will be able to do a great deal of work right on our own lot instead of going out on locations away from the studio. It has also been necessary to establish a Miniature department which had been closed down for the past two years, so that we can make necessary trick equipment which we are using in the comedies now in the course of production, and which you will see on the screen when the comedies are shipped to you, such as trick ducks, horses, carriages, miniature sets, etc.

I was pleased that you liked *Romance of Cow Hollow* and *Wilderness Trail*, especially *Wilderness Trail*, for this was a picture that the director, Tom Mix, and I were lukewarm on it when we shipped it to New York, for we did not believe it came up to previous Mix pictures.

With reference to the Mix picture, *High Speed*, and the disapproval it met with when you reviewed it, I wish to say as follows: Before LeSaint began photographing on this picture he, Tom Mix, and myself felt that the scenario was one of the best that we had ever made with Mix and we all also felt that it would make the best picture that Mix had yet made up to date, and when we reviewed the completed picture we still felt of the same opinion — that it was the greatest Mix picture to date and we all congratulated ourselves on having made such a picture. I personally looked at the completed picture three times to see if it could be cut down as it was longer than the usual Mix picture, and in no way could I see where we could cut a foot of the film. In permitting LeSaint to start on this picture, I did so after careful reading and discussion of the scenario, and after I was thoroughly convinced in my own mind that it was a good scenario and suitable for Mix.

I do not know how Leo is under the impression that *High Speed* was a book, and that it was originally read in Los Angeles and that I requested that you buy it. If there ever was a book known as *High Speed*, I don't remember ever having read it, and if I ever did read it, it was so long ago that I entirely forgot about it. At any rate, one thing is certain, the story *High Speed* that was made with Mix was not from a book but was an original story written by a man in Los Angeles whom I engaged especially for that purpose. I will recite to you briefly how the story came to be written:

During the month of April of this year there was held in the City of Santa Monica near Los Angeles, an automobile road race. It happened that we had one of our cameramen there to photograph the race. An unfortunate accident occurred: in making a fast turn an automobile turned over, killed the driver, but the mechanic was unhurt. Our cameraman was just where this accident took place and photographed the entire accident. When I saw this film on the screen I believed that we had a valuable piece of film and conceived the idea of working it into a picture for Mix, the picture to be a sporting picture and the auto accident to be the climax of the film. I talked the matter over with Mix and LeSaint and we all agreed such a story would be an excellent vehicle for Mix. I then engaged a writer by the name of Van Loan (H.H.), in Los Angeles, to write the story. Therefore, *High Speed* was not from a book purchased by the New York office at my request, but an original story written here.

It was my opinion that there was a sufficient love interest in it with a good part for the girl. Regarding the prize fight in the picture, that was my own idea, and I will admit that I "stole" it from one of the most successful acts that played the vaudeville theaters of the country about ten years ago. At that time I remember there was a sketch produced by Bernard Granville, entitled *Star Bout*, which played all the biggest vaudeville theaters of the country for about three years. It was a prize fight act, where the girl, dressed in boy's clothes attends the fight and prevents her sweetheart who is one of the fighters, from being doped. This sketch I remember made a big hit, and I figured if such a sketch could play for three years in theaters where fifty percent of the audiences are women, it would surely meet favor in a motion picture. I also had in mind Maurice Tournier's* [sic] picture *Sporting Life* which was such a big success recently. In this picture the principal thing was a prize fight supposed to be held at the National Sporting Club of London. When I reviewed this picture at the theater, half the audiences were composed of women and they almost went crazy about it. It was the biggest thing in the picture, and I felt it would be a big success in our picture and would not meet with disfavor with the women in the audiences.

*Maurice Tourneur, one of the outstanding directors of the period.

Now, regarding the Brockwell picture *Gypsy* and the Tom Mix picture *Coming of the Law*, which you returned here to be rearranged and improved so that they could be made possible for release, I wish to call the following to your attention:

The original cost of the Brockwell picture was $16,595.54, and the cost of remaking it was $24,951.12: therefore, the cost of remaking it was larger than the original. On *Coming of the Law* the original cost was $45,829.26 and the cost of re-arranging it was $15,688.87, or one-third of the original cost. As to the necessity of remaking the Brockwell picture, I wish to call your attention to the following correspondence that I had with you before you went to Europe:

On October 31st, 1918, after I sent you the first revised version of the story you wired me as follows:

"Have read revised version Brockwell story consists of hackneyed idea used in pictures done ten years ago suggest that modern vehicle be created which would warrant putting this picture in Victory program."

I then had written a new version of the story which I sent you on February 20th, and on March first you wired me as follows:

"Read revised synopsis of *Sneak* first half of story seems padded and drags last half has sufficient action stop I doubt whether there will be any scenes in previous picture which will fit this synopsis stop greatest difficulty with previous picture was the two terrible men artist and his friend they necessarily would spoil any picture they were in stop if these men are not to be used revised synopsis approved providing first half of story is strengthened and padding removed."

In view of your instructions that the two men in the first picture who played the artist and friend not be used, it was necessary to engage two other men and remake practically four fifths of the picture, especially in order to build up and strengthen the plot and story; and in view of the fact that it would cost practically the same amount of money to remake four fifths as it would to make an entire new picture, I consented to let the director make an entire new picture feeling that in that case we would still have the original picture intact. I felt that your telegram to me of March first in which you approved of the second revised synopsis with the suggestions you made, gave me the necessary authority to go ahead on the picture, especially as you felt doubtful as to whether we could use any of the scenes of the first version in the new synopsis.

Regarding *Coming of the Law* picture, only about one third of this picture was remade, to my recollection. When I originally made preparations to rearrange it, I figured on having about ten days work, but it was necessary to get the girl who played the lead in the first version. When I tried to get her, I found she was under contract to another company for six months, and although I tried everything possible to get her to finish the picture I was unable to do so, unless I would have been willing to wait for about four months. This was during the month of April and the picture was slated for release in May, and Leo and Sheehan both wrote me telling me of the necessity of having this picture ready for May release. I could not wait for four months to get the girl, and I therefore had to get another girl and remake all the scenes in which the girl appeared. Although we remade only one-third of the picture, it took us three weeks to do it due to our encountering about one week of rain and fog at the time. To my recollection the only scenes remade in *Coming of the Law* were the love scenes between Tom and the girl, eliminating the train. I wrote you on February 11th regarding *Coming of the Law* and its changes, but at that time I did not think it would be necessary to change all the scenes with the girl.

Regarding the Brockwell picture *Sadie*, it is my hope that after you have reviewed the last three reels of this picture you will have changed you opinion of it. I thought it was a good human, heart interest, western story with humor, pathos and tragedy. My recollection of the first two reels is that the man she is engaged to marry is already married, and in her anger and disappointment decides to leave her home town and go out on the desert. We tried to confine all of the comedy in the picture to the other characters of the story, for in all the stories we prepare with Miss Brockwell we try not to give her any comedy characterization.

With reference to our outstanding liability, which at the time of the writing of your letter was approximately seventy thousand dollars, and which is now approximately sixty-five thousand dollars, I desire to call your attention to the fact that out of the money that was wired to the William Fox Vaudeville Company, Los Angeles, during the latter part of March, the month of April and the early part of May, we paid out approximately $15,000 for bills which were taken over by the William Fox Vaudeville Company. We also carry on our books purchases of stories amounting to $9,000, which will be made into future pictures. This sum of money was paid out of the weekly remittances to the William Fox Vaudeville Company here. The principal purchases are for stories purchased for Farnum, namely *Joyous Trouble Makers* and *When the Desert Shall Bloom*, amounting to $4,500. In other words the total of this item and the amount we paid out for Sunshine Comedies, In. amounted to $24,000 which is the reason for the large outstanding liability.

With reference to Gilstrom's picture that he made here entitled *Smiles* costing $34,000, or twice as much as the two pictures he made in New York, I wish to call to your attention that during the making of this picture Jane Lee was sick and unable to work for three weeks, so that during that period of her illness practically no work was done in the picture and we were compelled to carry the entire cast and company on our payroll. In fact, I wrote you at the time whether you wanted the picture finished without Jane Lee. When Gilstrom came to Los Angeles he told me that you had authorized him to make any changes in the scenario he saw fit, which was verified by you in your letter of October 10th to me. There were at least three sequences that he photographed that did not appear in the picture due to the fact that the picture was greatly over-length. This was one of the other big reasons for the high cost. As to the man himself regarding his arrogance and actions and the fact that he refused to listen to me, all of which Sheehan, who was here at the time, knows about, this was the third principal reason for the extravagant cost of the picture.

Regarding the cost of the picture made with Peggy Hyland, Madelaine Traverse and Gladys Brockwell:

It seems that I have been unfortunate in being unable to get a director for Hyland who can make economical pictures. Every director I have had with her here, with the exception of Lawrence, we were compelled to dispense with due to the high cost of production such as Lynn Reynolds and Dowlan (William). So far Lawrence has made the best record. I have gone into this matter with Kingston in great detail. The technical cost of the Hyland pictures have been below the average cost of the sets in your Los Angeles Studio, as follows:

Miss Adventure	$43,320
Cowardice Court	$ 3,250
Bed She Made	$ 2,870
Girl with No Regrets	$ 3,100
Rebellious Bride	$ 3,400

The main reason for the high cost of the Hyland pictures is that it has taken us from five to five and a half weeks to photograph them. The present picture being made by Lawrence entitled *The Merry Go Round* will be photographed in four weeks, and I am in hopes it will cost not more than $22,000.

With reference to the Traverse pictures, these are made by Millarde in the best time possible, with the most careful supervision. The principal reason for the high cost of *Gambling In Souls* was because we had to charge to this picture $2,300 for Miss Traverse's salary for a period of seven weeks during which she did not work — four weeks during the Influenza layoff which she insisted upon being paid for, and the other three weeks waiting for the director. I have tried in every way possible to keep down the cost of the sets of the Traverse pictures. They have been, with the exception of one, society stories which require fairly good sets, but our records show that all of the sets in the pictures made with her have been of the average cost of the sets in the pictures made here. The technical cost is as follows:

Gambling In Souls	$3,150
Love That Dares	$3,340
When Fate Decides	$3,700
Until Eternity	$3,600

By the cost of the sets I mean the cost of carpenters, grips, electricians, painters and laborers.

The present Traverse picture being made by director Mitchell (Howard) is now complete. From the figures I have before me it will cost approximately $18,000.

I greatly appreciate the paragraphs in you letter wherein you absolve me of blame for the cost of *Evangeline* and the picture now being made by Gordon Edwards.

I appreciate what Millarde told you about me regarding the studios here. There is nothing that Millarde could have said otherwise that would have been the truth, for Millarde is the one man I worked with heart and soul on his stories, his pictures, during the making and cutting, to make them successful productions. I always had a great personal friendship for Millarde, but I never let that friendship interfere in any way with business. As to whether Millarde made the statements to you based on the assumption that he would one day return to Los Angeles again to make pictures in the studio here, I beg to call your attention to my letter to Jack Leo dated June 7th when I wrote him about Millarde returning to New York. In this letter I mentioned to Leo that I would much prefer if he could arrange to have Millarde remain in New York. When Millarde left Los Angeles he and I were personally on good terms, but not regarding our ideas on business.

I took exactly the same action with the directors who made the Hyland pictures as I did with Millarde. Lynn Reynolds, who was a director with Hyland in the second and third pictures she made here, I was compelled to discharge due to the fact he refused to work in cooperation with me. This took place while you were in Europe, and I wrote Jack Leo giving him all the circumstances as to why it was necessary for me to discharge him.

Likewise, with director Dowlan, who made *Cowardice Court* and who originally came here with the reputation of having made the fastest and cheapest pictures for the Triangle Film company, and whom I was compelled to stop from making additional scenes when I found out his method of working.

As you requested, I have made a comparison of the Hyland pictures made here and the Mix pictures made here, and I find that the five Hyland pictures cost, on an average, $29,200; and the twelve Mix pictures (not including *Coming of the Law*) cost on an average, $33,500.

Regarding the cost of the Lawrence picture *The Bed She Made*, it took

Lawrence five weeks to photograph this picture. You have already written me how fast Lawrence worked in New York, and Kingston has likewise told me the same here, but since Kingston has arrived it has been necessary for me to take up with him the slow way in which Lawrence is working, and I have several times talked to Lawrence telling him of the necessity of his being able to work much faster and I am on his toes practically every day.

In one of the paragraphs you refer to the salaries we paid to the people of the cast of the Hyland picture Lawrence made entitled *The Bed She Made*. You refer to Harry Hilliard to whom we paid $200. and while in New York three years ago received $100. a week when he was under contract. Hilliard has been in Los Angeles for about a year and during that time his salary has been $200. and $250. a week. It is practically impossible to get a leading man for less than $200. a week in Los Angeles. Right now, we are compelled to pay a man playing opposite Hyland a salary of $300. His name is Jack Mulhall. He was the only man available to suit the part. I know this is an outrageous salary, but all the studios here are in a position where our hands are tired, unless we are willing to do what other studios are doing and that is, place people under contract or in stock and thereby getting reductions in salaries.

According to our records here, the following is the supporting cast of the Hyland picture *The Bed She Made*:

Harry Hilliard, leading man	$200
William Elmoer, burglar-butler	100
Molly McConnel, mother	100
Mrs. Jack Mulhall, played part Hyland's sister	75
Ed Tilton, girl's father	75
E. Jobson, secretary	100
Ruth Hanford, minor part	50
Total supporting cast	$770

This is one of the cheapest supporting casts we have had for a long time. The woman you refer to as having received $300 a week and who in your opinion was only worth $10 a day, according to our records received only $75 a week. The name of this woman is Mrs. Jack Mulhall. Regarding the other actors in the cast such as the burglar, old man and the father, whom you mention are not worth more than $100 a week, were only paid $100 a week, the father getting only $75.

With reference to the four reasons you mention as being the principal causes for the high cost of the Brockwell, Traverse and Hyland pictures:

FIRST, the pictures being 20 percent too long—

I am enclosing herewith a list showing the length of the Excel pictures, likewise the Brockwell and Mix pictures that have been made here for the past ten months. This list shows that the average length of all of these pictures has been approximately 4,545 feet. The scenarios that we prepare here rarely run more than 220 to 230 scenes, and where they do run beyond that number it is because the director usually requests that all the close-ups be written in the scenario. My explicit instructions to the directors at all times have been that the Excel pictures made here, likewise the Victory pictures, are not to run beyond 4,300 or 4,400 feet and less if possible.

SECOND, regarding the sets used —

In preparing the sets for the various pictures it has been my endeavor to keep them down as much in cost as possible, but at all times to have sets suitable to the story. Traverse pictures, all of which except one having been society stories, required sets a little more elaborate than those used in Hyland pictures. However, in none of the pictures made with Traverse have we used large numbers of people, in these sets limiting them to not more than twelve people in one set. At all times, we make use of our own furniture wherever possible. However, our own supply of furniture is limited and we are compelled to go outside and rent most of our props. Some of our directors have a habit of trying to overcrowd their sets, however, I have now got them around to my way of thinking and that is, that a set always looks better on the screen if it has less furniture.

Due to the fact that we have such large stage room and we are able to place our cameras at a greater distance away from the set than we would in a smaller studio, most of our sets in my opinion appear larger on the screen than they really are.

With regard to using the same sets for different pictures, I have tried to do this wherever possible. In *Romance of Cow Hollow* we had a very large set which we used in the last three comedies that were made, *Wild Waves and Women*, *Yellow Dog Catcher* and *Chicken a la Cabaret*, which you have no doubt noticed; and we have since remade this set for a new comedy. A hotel lobby set that we erected for the Ray* picture *Love Is Love* we are using for a comedy now in work. A log cabin set which was used in the Traverse picture *Until Eternity* was used in *Romance of Cow Hollow* and in *Evangeline*; likewise in a comedy now being made. The sets that will appear in the new Traverse picture called *Splendid Sin* have been remade and used in the same picture over again with a slight change for a new picture with Ray.

All of these were sets that were on our stages when Kingston arrived and which I showed to him.

THIRD, regarding the casts that we have for the various pictures —

---

*Albert Ray, leading man.

I do all of the casting myself, that is, every person who is engaged for a picture whose salary amounts to more than $75 a week is personally approved by myself. The fact that we have to pay higher salaries for supporting casts than in New York is due solely to the conditions that exist here. The demand greatly exceeds the supply, therefore not only we but every other studio is in the position where we have to pay practically what is demanded of us. Other studios have in some measure overcome this by carrying a great number of actors and actresses in stock, thereby being able to somewhat save salaries. But we have never been able to carry out this policy, for in the past when we did carry people in stock and under contract we found that it did not work out to our advantage.

For example, in casting our new picture with Hyland today we required a juvenile man to play opposite her. The director recommended a young man who asked $250 a week. Mr. Kingston had a talk with him and offered him $150 which he refused. He then offered him $200 which he refused and refused to work for less than $250 which we refused to pay him, and therefore did not engage him. This particular man had not worked for six months and refused to work for less than the sum he asked. This is the general attitude nearly of all the actors in Los Angeles.

In your letter you mention that in examining the cast of the Hyland pictures you found it was necessary for us to pay $300 for a woman to play opposite Miss Hyland, and $250 for a man. I assume you refer to the picture *Cowardice Court*. On examining the payrolls of this picture, I find that the woman who played with Miss Hyland received $250 a week. Her name is Katherine Adams, and to this same woman, when she played with Farnum a year ago, we paid $150. Since then her salary has jumped to $250. She was the only woman who was available at the time who suited the part, and rather than hold up the picture, which would have meant a greater cost, we were compelled to engage her. On checking up I find she had been receiving $250 from the Lasky, Metro and Goldwyn Studios. Likewise we were compelled to pay Bertram Grassby* $250 a week in this picture although this man had been receiving from us $100 when he was under contract. $250 I find on investigation, is the salary he is now getting from other studios.

Actors and actresses to whom we were paying $100 and $150 a week a year ago and two years ago, are now getting double that money. I have gone into this matter with great thoroughness with Sam Kingston and he has made a careful investigation, and he has already told me that he did not think it will be possible for him to get the people here any cheaper than we are now getting them. In selecting our casts we try only to get the people suitable for the parts, and we try to get them as cheaply as possible.

*Leading man.

FOURTH, *with reference to the expensive rental prices paid for the hiring of furniture and props:*

This is a thing that is beyond my control. That is, we have to submit to the demand of the merchants in town who rent these goods. There are in the City of Los Angeles not more than six merchants who rent props for studios, and these merchants seem to have a working agreement, for if we turn down the goods of one merchant on account of high prices and go to another one, we are compelled to pay practically the same price. We have overcome this somewhat by using some of our own furniture which was purchased for us in New York about a year ago, and some which we have made ourselves, which is, however, totally insufficient for our demands at present.

In checking up some rental bill recently, I found that the merchants were charging us 20 percent more rental for the same goods that were used a year ago, and on communicating with them about it their reason was that they were compelled to advance their rental prices on account of the increase in the price of every other commodity.

This department has always had my personal attention. We rent nothing except when it is absolutely necessary. None of our people are permitted to go and rent props or furniture unless it is first okayed by me or my assistant.

There is at present a movement taking place in the Motion Picture Producers Association whereby they contemplate organizing a Central Purchase and Rental Bureau, that is have the producers appoint a committee to buy merchandise in bulk, like furniture and props, and rent it out to the producers. This if it goes through, will probably have a tendency to somewhat change the rental proposition. Every other studio in Los Angeles is in exactly the same position we are in. They have to pay the demands made by the merchants whose attitude is, "if you don't want the goods at our price you don't have to take them."

With reference to overhead:

The overhead for the past six months, with ten companies in operation, has averaged from $4,500 to $5,000, which is the lowest overhead that your Los Angeles studios have ever had. I showed all our records to Kingston with reference to this. Although we have doubled the number of companies operating a year ago, our increase in overhead has only been 20 percent. You will find attached herewith two charts marked #1 and #2.

Chart #1 shows overhead per picture on the pictures made during the period of February 1, 1919 to date when ten companies were operating, showing that the overhead per picture was $3,100. (I refer only to the Victory and Excel pictures, and not the Farnum pictures.)

Chart #2 shows that during the period from November 1, 1917 to

February 1, 1919 for similar pictures, when we had from three to five companies in operation, the overhead for each picture was $4280. In other words, there has been a decrease of $1180 per picture in the item of overhead, or 27½.

Regarding the cost of automobiles:

In my letter to you of June 19th, I went into great detail on this item. There is nothing else that I can say at this time other than what I have already written you about the matter. We have a system in our automobile department whereby every penny that is spent is accounted for, and no car is rented or given out for any purpose unless it is absolutely necessary. I have shown Mr. Kingston from our automobile records that we are operating our own automobiles at a far lower cost than we could go and rent these cars for, and that we have derived a profit from operating our own cars.

I wish to make one more remark with reference to the cost of sets and to the employment of the people who are engaged in the erection of sets. Before the sets for a picture are put up, our technical department makes up from the scenario a list of the sets required. This list is submitted to me and is approved by me before the work is commenced on the sets, so that we know approximately how much money the sets will cost at the finish of the picture. This refers to carpenters and laborers only. We still have the item of electricians and grips which are charged to the technical cost. This item depends upon the length of time it takes the director to photograph the picture, for grips and electricians work right along with the director. We have two grips and one electrician with each company, and we estimate that the labor of the electrician and grips amounts to about 15 percent of the total technical cost of each picture.

Every other day I go over our list of help with our technical department and lay off the people who are not needed, so that we employ only the number of people that we actually need.

With reference to Mr. Kingston coming here to help me out with some of my work, I wish to say that since I have been here I was never happier than when Mr. Kingston arrived, as I always am when anyone from New York comes out here. Mr. Kingston has already been of great help to me. When I consider that I have been here practically two years and that during that time Mr. Kingston is the first man that you have sent out here, outside of Mr. Sheehan, to look over your studios and to see what has actually been done, and when I realize that in the other studios in Los Angeles the heads or high executives come out to see them two or three times a year, you can greatly appreciate how happy I was that you sent Mr. Kingston out. I know that when he goes back to New York he can tell you more about your studio in thirty minutes than I could in a hundred page letter.

With reference to my being over-burdened with work, the more work I have the happier I am. I have never yet complained as to being over-burdened with work. I always felt that if at any time I found the job was getting beyond me I would be the first to write you. I have told Kingston that I want him to help me in every possible way that he can see.

I do not believe there is anyone who knows better than I how vital and important it is to make the pictures of the Excel program at a cost of between $18,000 and $20,000 so as to enable the Fox Film Corporation to earn a profit. The only thing I can see is that I have done everything that I can possibly do to accomplish this. I feel that the Ray picture which is a subject you did not mention in your letter, can easily be made within that sum. Sometimes a picture may run a little over; sometimes less, but the average cost will be between $18,000 and $20,000. In fact, of the four Ray pictures we have made to date, namely:

Married In Haste	$21,989
Be a Little Sport	21,489
Works and Music	20,312
Love Is Love	16,000

the average is $20,000.

The four items of sets, supporting casts, length of pictures and rental, overhead and automobiles will as usual, have my very careful attention, and if there is any possibility of the pictures being made between $18,000 and $20,000 in Los Angeles, I will make them. I have made so many promises in the past regarding the cost of pictures, all of which I have been unable to fulfill, that I do not want to make any promises now. But if the pictures that are made with Hyland and Traverse until September first do not average $18,000 to $20,000, I do not think we will be able to make them for that sum, for right now we are having the most wonderful weather, and fortunately we are able to get our stories in advance.

With reference to the second paragraph on page #12 of your letter, I wish to say that in my opinion *my manners and habits have not changed one iota from the day I left your office in New York.*

I note your paragraph with reference to loaning Tom Mix $2,500. Mix came to me one day and told me that he had an opportunity of buying a house immediately and needed $2500, and wanted to know if the company would loan it to him. He needed this money on short notice and I told him that I did not think the company would have any objection and arranged to loan him that sum. I wrote Jack Leo the same day. I realize that I made a serious mistake in not wiring you for your approval. The only thing I can say is that it was a "bonehead" piece of business and judgment on my part. I did not loan him the money without first securing your approval because I wanted to go beyond what I was privileged to do.

I felt at the time that I was doing it for the best interest of the company, and I realized soon after the transaction that I should have wired for your approval.

I know that you have given me probably the biggest opportunity that anyone can ask for, and I feel that there is no one in your entire organization who is working harder than I am to appreciate what you have done.

With reference to Bach coming to Los Angeles, I feel that I should leave that entirely up to Mr. Kingston. I feel that there is nothing that Bach can do to help us in the technical department, for it is running at the most economical basis possible. I told Mr. Kingston that if he felt it would relieve your mind to have Bach out here and supervise our technical department for as long a period as you wanted him to, I would be more than pleased. Kingston, however, agreed with me that he saw nothing that Bach can do that will in any way improve the present condition.

The other day I took Mr. Kingston to a meeting of the Motion Picture Producers Association and had him meet the representatives of practically all the other studios in Los Angeles, and during the meeting he discussed with them the various subjects with reference to the various items in the production of pictures. Mr. Kingston told me that he would write you of the information he gained so that you would know exactly what the other studios are doing.

With reference to the present picture being made with Mix, *The Hard Boiled Tenderfoot*, and which is being directed by Mix himself, I wish to say that when LeSaint contemplated going east our arrangements were that while he was away Mix was to photograph his stunt scenes and LeSaint was to finish the picture on his return. Mix, in the meantime, was to work in co-operation with LeSaint's assistant, George Webster. Mix began photographing the picture two or three days after LeSaint left. I had written Leo previously to this effect. LeSaint was gone four weeks and returned Saturday, July 12th. Mix will be through photographing with his picture about July 18th, so that there is nothing that LeSaint can really do on it. It was distinctly understood, however, between Mix and myself that the picture was to be co-directed with George Webster who I felt would be able to do good work, as he is a bright and intelligent man. If Mix has in any way made claims to you that he himself directed *Romance of Cow Hollow* he is not stating facts, although it is true that Mix and I were compelled to go over the work with the director every day and line up his work, and practically introduce all of the material that is at present in the picture. However, every scene that is in *Romance of Cow Hollow* was directed by the man whose name appears on the screen as the director.

You will probably realize from the correspondence that has passed between us regarding Mix that he is a vastly different man than when you knew him and than he was six or eight months ago. Mix during that period has never been satisfied with anything or anyone. He is always talking about being his own director and that no director understands him. In this last statement he is probably correct, for some of the directors we have had with Mix feel that they know more than Mix does about the kind of work he does, in which they are wrong, for I do not believe there is a director in the entire Motion Picture business who can teach Mix about the West or about the kind of stunts that Mix should do. The only director who has been able to get along with Mix fairly well has been LeSaint and Mr. LeSaint's attitude is that he would much prefer not to direct him.

The main difficulty with Mix regarding directors has been that as soon as he gets a new director whom he cannot control and tell what to do, he has no use for him. That is the reason we discontinued Reynolds from making pictures with him; and Rosson (Arthur H.) who directed *Romance of Cow Hollow.* Likewise with LeSaint, who I have arranged according to my present plans, to direct the next Mix picture and who would rather that he did not direct it.

I have read to Mix your entire paragraph regarding the engaging of the best director available for him. There are two difficulties regarding this, the first being that although I have looked over the entire market of directors in Los Angeles who are not under contract, I did not find one director who I feel would be capable of making pictures with Mix. Second, if we were able to get a really good honest-to-God-director who would work for the interest of the company and not a man who always wants to make "director's pictures", and pay him a salary of from $750 to $1,000 a week (this is the salary that so-called "good" directors are asking in Los Angeles), such a director would usually insist that he be the director of the company, which is a thing that Mix would not be able to stand for more than a week or two, as it is against his nature, as I have above stated. This is a matter that Mix and I have talked and argued about for months. I hope that during the time LeSaint is making the next picture with Mix I will be able to get a director who will be suitable to Mix and who I feel can make good pictures with him.

Mr. Kingston showed me the article which appeared in the magazine of the Sunday World and after reading same I immediately dismissed Marc Robbins without notifying him as to the reason thereof. At the present time I am taking care of the Scenario Department myself inasmuch as I have been unable to find anyone In Los Angeles who I feel is capable of supervising it.

The hapless Mr. Robbins, head of the Fox west coast Scenario Department, had been guilty of allowing himself to be interviewed at length by journalist Karl K. Kitchener during a visit to the studio.

Entitled "Why Movie Scenarios Are What They Are" and captioned "The Story Writing Department in a film studio is tolerated as a necessary Evil, the problem being to make the scenarios fit the Star," Kitchener's article was printed in the New York Sunday World *on June 22, 1919; goaded Mr. Fox into action on the 23rd; and was delivered to Wurtzel on June 30, thereby causing Robbins to be fired precipitously on July 1.*

Unfortunately for Robbins, Kitchener chose to write the interview in a flippant, ironical style, and if Robbins was faithfully quoted, he was equally responsible for his own downfall. Kitchener described the story editor as "ruling supreme, except when Jove-like, Mr. William Fox interferes."

Robbins blamed the public for poor moving pictures. "No, don't blame the scenarios. We can't help it if the public prefers a pretty boy or a 'chicken' to a competent actor or actress." Then he described the tortuous metamorphosis of a good script into a mediocrity:

"a workmanlike scenario is prepared for the newest actor who has been discovered by the President of a film company in a manicure parlor in Boston or Philadelphia, for stars are made by the Presidents even as they are made by theatrical managers; the scenario is sent to the star for approval — for when a film President is paying anyone a large salary, he naturally wants his or her opinion, whether it is worth anything or not.

"Miss Maybelle Meringue or whatever her name is, reads the scenario and suggests several changes in order to make herself more important — then it is passed along to her personal manager — the high-priced director — when he gets through shooting the picture, the only things left are the title and names of the characters."

Kitchener asked if then there was no ray of sunshine in his life. When Robbins answered that there would be better pictures someday "not in my time or your time, but in the sweet bye and bye" he did not know how prophetic he was being. William Fox promptly saw to it that it wouldn't be in his reign.

Referring back to the item of the cost of pictures, on page #8 of your letter you mention that in examining the cost of Gordon Edwards pictures you find that of 20 performers in the company he has 15 of these whose salaries do not average over $75 a week. In explanation of this I would like to say that of these 15 performers whose salaries do not average more than $75 a week, 10 or 12 of them are cowboys whom we pay $30 to $35 and who are usually paid day by day by "extra" check. But when the Edwards company leaves for location to stay away for three or four weeks at a time we put these cowboys on weekly salary. These cowboys cannot really be termed performers, as on examining the Mix payroll I find that we likewise have with Mix about 10 cowboys that we carry on weekly salaries and who ordinarily should be classed as extras, and should be paid $7.50 per day. We only carry these cowboys on weekly salary who are the pick of the field and who have worked with us for a long time, so that we can keep them with us permanently and not let another company take them away from us.

I find that in almost every instance the weekly cost of the Edwards payroll, that is the salary of the director and his staff and all his artists, without Farnum's salary, has been greater than the weekly payroll of any other company we have in Los Angeles including the star.

I am enclosing herewith the following charts: "A" being the comparison of cost of the Mix and Hyland pictures which I have taken up in one of my preceding paragraphs:

#3 is a list of the pictures (not including Farnum, Bara or Standard pictures), made from the day the Los Angeles studio opened to November 1, 1917, showing 23 pictures made at an average cost of $27,300.

#2 shows pictures made during the period from November 1, 1918 to February 1, 1919, during which time we had from three to five companies operation. Thirty-one pictures were made (not including Farnum, Bara or Standard pictures), at an average cost of $27,000. The average technical cost per picture was $3,400 and the average Los Angeles overhead per picture was $4,280.

Chart #1 shows that during the period from February 1, 1919 to date when we had ten companies operating, we made 15 pictures (not including Farnum pictures) at an average cost of $27,500. The technical cost per picture was $3,600 and Los Angeles overhead was $3,100 per picture. With reference to this chart I wish to call to your attention that we have included the most expensive Mix pictures made to date, namely, *Romance of Cow Hollow*, *High Speed* and *Wilderness Trail* on which pictures we have knowingly spent additional money.

The pictures which appear on charts #1 and #2 were made during the time I have been in you Los Angeles studios. Included in the cost of these pictures, which does not appear in the sort of pictures made prior to November 1, 1917, are the following items:

New York overhead amounting to $57,911 or an average of $960 per picture.

Depreciation amounting to $121,786.27 or an average per picture of $1,964.

Total of both items per picture $2,924.

In other words, if these two items are to be figured as a separate item from the cost of the pictures made from November 1, 1917 to date as a comparison to the pictures made prior to November 1, 1917, the average cost per picture would be about $24,600 or a decrease of $2,700 per picture.

The item of New York overhead is an item that is charged to us each week by the New York office and I do not know exactly how it is made up. We are instructed every week by the New York auditor to charge to each production a certain amount known as New York Overhead.

The item of Depreciation, amounting to $121,786 represents studio equipment such as electrical supplies, cameras, properties, buildings, etc. that we purchased or erected during the period from November 1, 1917 to date and which would are now at the studio and included in our inventories, and which would still have approximately the same value now that they had when they were purchased, but are charged off to the productions every four weeks.

I also wish to call your attention to an item which has appeared every week on our pay rolls for the past 20 months marked stock talent as follows: Francis Carpenter; Virginia Lee Corbin; Melvin Messenger; Violet Radcliff whose total combined salaries amount to $ a week. Of these children we have practically no benefits, using them in scenes where we need children and who we could ordinarily get for $3 to $5 a day. This item is distributed weekly among the pictures in production.

Below I am giving you four memorandums showing the difference in the cost of labor, the cost of lumber, paints and hardware which are the principal items used in the erection of our sets.

	Prior to Oct. 1917	*Oct. 1917–Oct.1918*	*Oct. 1918 to date*
Grips	$18 to $21 wkly	$24 wkly	$30 wkly
Painters	$18–$21–$24	30	36
Carpenters	$21	30	36
Props	$18–$21	24–25	2–35
Electricians	$21–$24	30	30
Laborers	$15	18	21
Carpenter Foreman	$31	36	39
Technical Director	$40	50	50–60

In other words, there has been an increase in wages of the people who are used in erection of sets since October 1917 or 66 percent.

Below I will give you the cost of the principal kinds of lumber used here:

<table>
<tr><td></td><td colspan="3" align="center">*Rough Oregon Pine*</td></tr>
<tr><td></td><td>*July 1917*</td><td>*July 1918*</td><td>*July 1919*</td></tr>
<tr><td>2 × 3</td><td>$30.00 per M</td><td>$34.50 per M$</td><td>42.50 per M</td></tr>
<tr><td>2 × 6</td><td>30.00</td><td>33.75</td><td>41.75</td></tr>
<tr><td>1 × 12</td><td>30.00</td><td>38.00</td><td>47.00</td></tr>
<tr><td>1 × 12 × 12</td><td>17.50</td><td>21.50</td><td>26.00</td></tr>
<tr><td></td><td colspan="3" align="center">*Clear Vertical Grain Surface 4 Sides*</td></tr>
<tr><td>1 × 4 × 3</td><td>56.00</td><td>68.50</td><td>91.00</td></tr>
<tr><td></td><td colspan="3" align="center">*Clear Redwood Surface 4 Sides*</td></tr>
<tr><td>1 × 12</td><td>55.00</td><td>56.50</td><td>67.00</td></tr>
</table>

This shows that there has been an increase in lumber during the period of the last two years of approximately 45 percent.

Below you will find a chart showing the relative cost of paints and oils two years ago and a year ago, also a memorandum from our purchasing agent, G.S. McEdwards showing there has been an increase in hardware of about 40 percent.

	Two Years Ago	One Year Ago	Now
Umber	5 1/2c lb	8c lb	8 1/2c lb
Sienna	5 1/2c lb	8 1/2c lb	9 1/2c lb
Shellac	1. 30 gal	2.35 Gal	3.50 gal
White Shellac	1.40 gal	2.50 Gal	3.60 gal
White Lead	8 1/2c lb	111c lb	12c lb
Drop Black	7c	12c	14c
Linseed Oil	.76	1.28	2.24
Turps	.54	.68	1.14
Glue	.26	.40	.60
Gold Bronze	.75	1.10	1.30
Oil Colors		2.09	2.59
Whiting	1 1/2c	.02	.02 1/2
Alcohol	.58	.48	.59
Japans	.68	.90	1.10
All dry colors		x20 percent	40 percent

The above items will show the enormous increase of everything pertaining to technical items that enter into the cost of our sets for the pictures, whereas charts #1 and #2 which give the technical cost of the pictures, will show that this item has practically remained stationary during the past two years.

I am unable to give you the technical cost of pictures made prior to November 1, 1917, for at that time the books of the studio were kept in a different way and the cost of the pictures were figured in a lump sum and were not distributed to the various items as we do now. The new system was put into effect about July, 1917.

With reference to material for our directors, I wish to say that we are greatly in need of stories for the following: Miss Hyland and Al Ray. We find it hardest to get suitable stories for these two people. We have been getting along fairly well with stories for Miss Traverse, Tom Mix and Miss Brockwell. However, I can always use all the material that can be submitted by New York. During the past, the Scenario Department in New York has been of wonderful help to us in keeping up with stories. However, I would suggest that a special effort be made to get material for Ray and Hyland.

I believe I have fully covered everything in your letter. I have read this entire letter to Mr. Kingston so that he is fully acquainted with the contents of same, for I have written this letter from day to day after going over with Mr. Kingston every item about which I have written.

I trust that you are well and will enjoy a very pleasant summer in your new country home about which Mr. Kingston has told me. I remain, with kindest regards,

Yours very truly,
SMW/AS

New York City
September 8, 1919

Mr. Sol M. Wurtzel
Los Angeles

My dear Sol:

This will serve to inform you that I have this day increased your salary to $200 per week. With kindest regards, I am,

Very truly yours,
(signed) William Fox

Los Angeles
September 27, 1919

(Copy)
Mr. William Fox
New York City

My dear Mr. Fox:

I wish to acknowledge your letter of September 8th wherein you advise me of my increase in salary, for which I sincerely wish to thank you. Also at this time I wish you and all those who are dear to you my best wishes for a bright and happy New Year.

Yours very truly,

New York City
October 27, 1919

Mr. S.M. Wurtzel
Los Angeles

My dear Sol:

I have reviewed the picture *The Feud*, also *Naughty Wink*. I am unwilling to express an opinion on either one of these two pictures because of their cost; *The Feud*, according to our records, being $69,346.67, with no

222

knowledge as to whether that is the completed cost or whether there is more to come; *Naughty Wink* $36,377.79, with no knowledge whether this is the cost of the picture, without any more to come — however, with the full knowledge that regardless of the quality of either one of these two stories, the Fox Film Corp. must and will lose money, for it cannot possibly get out, in rentals, the cost of either one of these two productions. It is enough to break a man's heart to think that he is working day and night in the hopes of trying to earn a fair profit or return on his investment, only to be confronted with costs, as above stated, which rob me of the possibilities of not only making a profit but guaranteeing a loss before I start.

Your explanation of this I already have from Sheehan about some trip which was taken so that the herd of buffaloes could be photographed in connection with *The Feud*, and I suppose the further alibi would be your inability to handle Mix. However, neither one of these two alibis are sufficient for me. You, as my representative, had authority to shut down on the making of this picture. It would have been far better never to have made it than to have made it at all this cost, and I cannot understand your attitude in permitting this gross violation to occur, and you are hereby ordered and instructed in the future never to permit it to happen again, without first receiving my consent from this end.

Your alibi in connection with the comedy will be, I presume, that you have no control over the expenditure; however you have control over the signature of money, and long before any such sum as this was expended, you should have wired me to ask my opinion on it. This comedy cost is caused by having supplied sufficient material in a two reel comedy for a five reel picture, and in my opinion, it was a willful effort to attain something, regardless of cost, which you must and should know that I am not interested in, for our company cannot exist unless it has a chance to get back the money which it expends.

This letter should serve notice on you for your future conduct in expending moneys belonging to me and the company, and I want an assurance from you that a re-occurrence of this will not and cannot possibly happen during your supervision of the Los Angeles Studios.

Yours truly,
(signed) William Fox

Los Angeles
November 3, 1919

(Copy)
Mr. William Fox
New York City

My dear Mr. Fox:

I wish to acknowledge your letter of October 22nd with reference to the picture *The Feud* and the comedy *Her Naughty Wink*.

With reference to the picture *The Feud*, I have no alibi to make regarding the cost. Mr. Kingston was here during the time this entire picture was photographed and was fully acquainted with all the circumstances in the making of this particular picture, and on the day he left he told me that he would tell you in person exactly what occurred to make the cost of this picture so excessive. The final and completed cost of the picture *The Feud* was $69,334, as stated in your letter.

Before LeSaint began working on this production, I figured out with him and also separately with Mr. Kingston that at the most this picture would cost from $40,000 to $45,000, taking into consideration the fact that LeSaint would have to make two location trips. If the picture had been made according to the plans outlined, it would not have cost over that amount. I am stating this because before every picture is started I sit down with the director and figure out exactly how such money should be expended on the picture.

The Feud was started by the company first going to location to photograph the buffalo episode. When the company came back from location I had a very long talk with Mr. Kingston and told him then that the picture, in view of the condition that existed and the unwillingness of Mix to co-operate with his director and with the corporation, would cost far more money than should be expended on it. I took up with him then as to whether it would not be advisable to notify you of the circumstances and to ascertain from you whether to continue with the pictures or permit the picture to be finished. If Mr. Kingston had not been here, I would certainly have communicated with you as I had done in the case of director Lawrence when he made the picture with Traverse, when I realized the Lawrence picture would cost more money than it should. However, Mr. Kingston being on the ground, and as I understood from him for this particular purpose, he told me that there was nothing that I could do other than what I was doing to expedite the finishing of the picture at the lowest possible cost, and that I should not cause you any undue worry by communicating the facts to you; that you fully understood the situation regarding Mix, as he had written you about it, and that the best thing to do was to finish the picture in the best possible way, and I agreed with Mr. Kingston on this.

Mr. Kingston knows that when the company came back from Oklahoma, I sat down with director LeSaint and eliminated an episode from the story that would have cost $15,000. to make, because I knew that the picture would cost so much money. This episode, from the original scenario which you have in New York, was a land rush which the company was supposed to have taken on location and which they did not get.

I am stating the above facts to you because I know how you feel about the matter and I now that there is no sense in making the pictures at a cost where you cannot derive a profit therefrom. However, I would also like you to know that this matter was constantly in my mind, and that the question I took up with Mr. Kingston was—whether it would be advisable to stop the making of the picture then and there, incurring possibly a loss of $25,000 or $30,000. which had already been spent in the preparation of the story and in the photographing of the scenes on location, or whether to have the picture completed in the best possible way, and Mr. Kingston advised me that he could not see where anything could be gained by stopping the picture and communicating with you and having to pay the salaries of the director, star and cast without work being accomplished.

While Mr. Sheehan was here and before he left, I took up with him the question of the costs of the future Mix pictures, and the maximum amount of money that should be spent. Mr. Sheehan explained in detail what material to put in the Mix pictures in the way of stunts, sets, characters, et., and I told him that I did not think we could make the future Mix pictures for less than $50,000; first because where we photographed the first Mix pictures made on an average of 4 weeks, they now take from 5 to 6 weeks to photograph; and also in view of Mix's increased salary* and the increased cost of the sets, etc. You will note that outside of *The Feud*, the last 3 Mix pictures made averaged $42,000.

Rough Riding Romance cost	$42, 858
The Dare Devil cost	42,286
The Speed Maniac cost	41, 727

All of the above without Mix's increased salary.

Mr. Sheehan told me that it will be satisfactory to you to have the Mix pictures cost about $50,000. The present Mix picture may run a few thousand dollars over the sum. This is due to the fact that we have in this picture a Chinese Street set of a peculiar character which has cost a large sum of money to build, and the stunts that take place in this set are of a very difficult nature to photograph and will take a great deal of time. This set and the stunts in this set were suggested by Mr. Sheehan when he was here.

The next Mix picture will be *3 Gold Coins* and is a continuation of the first reel of *Rough Riding Romance*. I do not think it will run over $25,000 because I am arranging with the director to photograph the story within 3 weeks.

*Mix was now getting $1500 per week.

It is not my desire to permit pictures to be made for quality only irrespective of the cost, for I know that no picture, no matter how good it is, is of any value to you unless a profit can be earned. My understanding of the cost of the brand of pictures that are being made in the Los Angeles Studios should be as follow:

Excel pictures from $20,000 to $22,000

Victory pictures from $25,000 to $27,000

Mix pictures, in accordance with Mr. Sheehans suggestion, $50,000

Comedies from $20,000 to $22,000.

The average cost of the 13 Excel pictures is $21,000 or very close to the amount you want expended on them. Therefore, if one or two pictures should run over that amount, when they are averaged up they will be within the cost set. There is absolutely no doubt in my mind that the average cost of the Excel pictures and the Victory pictures that will be made, will be within the amounts you have set for them.

With regard to the Mix pictures, all I want from him is a fifty-fifty break, and if he gives me only 50 percent of the co-operation that he gave the first year and a half when he made feature pictures, his pictures will cost within the amount you want. I can assure you that Mix's actions during the picture *The Feud* and the few pictures previous to that have caused me so much worry knowing that all this has caused the cost of his pictures to go up, without results being obtained, in fact enough worry to make a man go off his mind. I told Sheehan about the entire situation and I hope he has told you about it, for then you will know about matters which I did not want to write you about because I did not want to worry or annoy you. However, in the future, as you state in your letter, if in any picture that Mix or any other picture where I see that by the actions of the star or director the picture will miss to excessive cost, I will stop the production and notify you.

With reference to the comedies, I went into this matter with Mr. Sheehan to a great extent, and I told him that unless DelRuth* made a radical change in his methods and not permit his directors to photograph indiscriminately but set a definite amount of time for each picture, we could never hope to make the comedies within the cost of $20,000 or $22,000. I told Sheehan that it was DelRuth's ambition to make comedies irrespective of cost so that DelRuth's name could be glorified. I came to this conclusion after a careful observation of DelRuth and his methods. Mr. Sheehan, however told me that he had many talks with him and had come to a full understanding with DelRuth who promised to make the comedies within the proper cost.

Hampton DelRuth — formerly with Keystone Comedies, he replaced Henry Lehrman as head of Fox's Sunshine Comedies.

I know that I have originally boosted and praised DelRuth, however after DelRuth had made the first 6 or 8 comedies, his methods changed and instead of making comedies for quality with a view of cost, he made them for quality only. In fact, I advised Sheehan that in order to protect you for the future, that a contract should be made with comedy director J.G. Blystone (John), which was done, for I consider Blystone one of the best comedy directors in the business. In fact, he had directed the best of the Sunshine comedies.

I enclose you herewith copy of a note I have this day sent to Mr. DelRuth after having a talk with him upon receiving your letter. The total and completed cost of the comedy *Her Naughty Wink* is $36,337 as stated in your letter.

With reference to the Shirley Mason* pictures, Mr. Sheehan, before he left, impressed on me very strongly to be sure that the Shirley Mason pictures should be of such a quality and nature so that they can, if possible, advance her out of the program class and put her into the Star Series class for next season; and that plenty of time should be spent in the preparation of the story and photographing. Also while en route to New York he wired me several times to be sure that the first Mason picture should be a knockout in every way and that from 6 to 8 weeks should be spent in the preparation of the story. Naturally, in order to take so much time for the preparation of the story and in the photographing, the picture will have to cost a good deal of money, and as my understanding is that her pictures should be in the Excel Program, they should not cost more than $22,000 and I cannot see how we can afford to take so much time for the preparation and photographing. The reason I am mentioning this is that if I am to follow out Mr. Sheehan's suggestion the picture will have to cost more than $22,000. As I have stated in my previous paragraph, the reason we were able to keep the Excel pictures down is because the directors were compelled to photograph them in three and three and a half weeks and take only about a week and a half off at the most between pictures. I am assuming that you do not want the Shirley Mason pictures to cost more than the above mentioned amount, and for that reason will not be able to give it the preparation and time that Mr. Sheehan requested should be done.

I have just received your letter of October 29th instructing me to stop all photographing on the Blystone #6 comedy, *The Great Nickel Robbery*. This picture was completed on October 25th and the total and completed cost of same was $31,795.

In conclusion I will reiterate what I have stated above, that if at any

---

*A petite, winsome brunette whom Fox was to star in Mary Pickford–like roles, with great success.

time in the future if by reason of the action of any director or star the picture will cost more money than is allotted to it, I will stop production and communicate with you by telegram immediately.

Very Truly yours,

New York City
November 6, 1919

Mr. S. M. Wurtzel
Los Angeles

My dear Sol:

On Nov. 5th, I sent you the following night telegram: "Sheehan reports that Coast Studios are working carefully and energetically on new productions which I am pleased to hear. With reference Mix next picture entitled *Three Gold Coins* you are using at least one thousand feet returned through Sheehan which was eliminated from *Rough Riding Romance* stop I consider the thousand feet returned you as excellent material when slightly snapped up and therefore you have at least the first reel of your *Three Gold Coin* Production. I absolutely insist upon a first class production to follow this first reel. Sheehan informs me that Vanloan has excellent material of real western merit with good story stop You have practically only three reels of the picture to produce therefore feel that expenditure twenty thousand dollars in addition to Mix salary should furnish us a corking good subject stop Wire me confirming what you consider maximum expenditure on balance of *Three Gold Coin* story besides first reel *Rough Riding Romance* not including Mix salary and if you are set."

I am relying on you to carry out the terms of this night telegram.

Sheehan has read to me the memorandum which was dictated in Mix's presence, in your office, which sets forth the complete understanding between you and Tom Mix. Sheehan has told me of the dirty, damnable conduct of Mix towards you. Personally, I doubt very much that had I been on the ground, I ever would have changed an iota of the old Mix contract. I would have compelled him to remain out of work rather than enter into new arrangement* after his behavior towards you. However, this has now been done, and the best interests of the Fox Film Corp. require that you and Tom Mix be close and intimate friends, if the Company is to continue to make pictures with him of the type and kind which the public will demand and at a cost which will enable us to earn a profit.

This new contract called for annual increases of $500 per week until $3,000 was paid by 1923, and cancellation of the $2,500 promissory note.

The high-handed manner of Mix as regards the expenditure of money belonging to the Fox Film Corp., in my opinion, is nothing short of a disgrace. You are responsible, for it began the day you loaned him $2,500 on your own account, without first receiving my sanction or the sanction of the directors of the Fox Film Corp., which I have already written you was a violation of your office. Therefore, I am warning you never to do it again. At the time you made this loan you expected to have it returned some day. You now see that as a result of the negotiations, the Fox Film Corp., is actually losing the $2,500. It is because he owed us $2,500, that he was able to figure some sort of a basis whereby the $2,500 was allowed to him. Sheehan explains it in a perfectly logical way. However, there would have been no explanation necessary if Mix did not owe me $2,500. Therefore, your loaning a man my money or money belonging to my company appeared as a loan when you made it, and now appears as having presented it, and of course you never had any such power.

I am writing this letter just to bring forcibly to your attention again the necessity of your actions being only of a type and kind which have been sanctioned by me, and that any variations from our strict, standard rules is unauthorized by me, and you are not permitted to go into any without first receiving my sanction either by telegraph or in writing, so that I may have it approved by the directors of the Fox Film Corp.

I am of the opinion that Mix will never like you any more than you like him. You, however, are supposed to have executive ability and should be able to hide your feelings, and let come to the surface only that which will best serve the interests of the Fox Film Corp. I feel that this letter is probably unnecessary, for I am sure that that was the plan which you had in mind, and that you expected to conduct yourself accordingly. I am mentioning it because since the contract with Mix was signed, I found no such promise from you in writing. Therefore I have assumed that the prejudice is still existing and would exist unless you received this communication.

Very truly yours,
(signed) William Fox

Publicity has always had it that in his heyday, Mix received anywhere from $10,000 to $17,000 a week from the Fox Corporation. In reality, his last contract written with Fox in 1925 called for a maximum of $7,500 and out of that he had to provide fodder for his co-star, Tony.

Following his boss's dictates and in the interest of the profits of the Fox Film Corp., Wurtzel swallowed Mix's insults but he never digested them. Instead, he groomed another cowboy, Charles "Buck" Jones, to compete with him. Never the box office draw that Mix was, Buck did build up a sizable following. He became very popular with the Saturday afternoon audiences in spite of Fox's personal opinion of his first picture, which follows:

New York City
December 9, 1919

Mr. S. M. Wurtzel
Los Angeles

My dear Sol:

I sent you the following night telegram:

"Reviewed Brockwell picture very good stop Also reviewed Buck Jones picture Impossible to release Worst amateurish direction I have ever reviewed Dismiss director immediately Hire someone else to complete present picture Will shelve picture we have here"

I was keenly and sadly disappointed in this picture, especially because of the great extraordinary effort that you had made in supervising this production so that it would be a great motion picture. Were it not for the fact that I knew it was your ambition to make Mix envious of the first picture that you made with Buck Jones, I would make every allowance for this picture, but in view of the fact that you were all keyed up to the point of making this a great picture, and most likely devoted tons and tons of time to it, and then upon the completion of it to have such a miserable, terrible, rotten affair as that, is beyond my understanding. I would like to blame the story for this imperfect picture, but I could see the possibilities in this story if it had been developed in proper scenario form, and if an intelligent director had directed it. I presume, by the time you receive this letter, this director will no longer by connected with the Company, and that you are locating someone else. We could never think of releasing this picture if we intend to retain the services of Buck Jones.

Very truly yours,
(signed) William Fox

By the year 1920, the Fox Film Corporation had eighty-four Exchanges and branch offices spread over the United States and all the important cities of the world. The lavish new headquarters and production plant on West 56th Street in New York City were completed in March and Fox moved into his vast, imposing new office. Surrounded by this aura of power and prosperity he continued to direct protestations of penury towards the West.

Wurtzel reluctantly admitted that running the studio single-handed was too much for one man and asked for someone to take over the business end so that he could devote more time to production. He complained that Fox's letters left him in a nervous condition and begged that a personal conference be arranged either in New York or Los Angeles but Fox found an excuse to postpone all requests. He was either informed, or sensed across a distance of thirty-five hundred miles, whenever his superintendent was forming a personal friendship with any of the studio writers or directors and would order them fired because he suspected they were influenc-

ing Wurtzel. This was particularly true with Edward LeSaint and Jules Furthman. Sometimes the younger man would resort to having an employee change his name so that he could be kept on the payroll.

Wurtzel's efforts to develop Omer Locklear, the World War I air ace, into a new Fox star met with tragic results; he made a more felicitous decision when he hired twenty-five year old John Ford to direct the Buck Jones pictures. William Fox too, was quick to recognize the young director's talents and over the years Ford was to direct fifty pictures for Fox Films and later, 20th Century–Fox. Four of them won Academy Awards: The Informer, Grapes of Wrath, How Green Was My Valley *and* The Quiet Man.

New York City
January 30, 1920

Mr. S.M. Wurtzel
Los Angeles,

My dear Sol:

Replying to your letter of January 21st, in which you analyze the various costs on Edwards-Farnum pictures made. There never was any doubt in my mind that you couldn't explain the whole thing in various ways— stating that pictures were made away on locations, that carpenters and actors had to be transported and many other such items that are easily explained, but of course are damn costly.

With the great facilities that we have in Los Angeles, why do we always keep on going away? Every time I criticize you for the extraordinary cost, it is always the same alibi —125 miles to location. What in the Hell is the use of having a commodious plant in Los Angeles if it is not to make pictures there? We have had a mighty serious Winter here; the weather this year was worse than any year that I can remember, and up to the time of this writing we have had no occasion for any director to go away. It is because of this we are able to keep our cost down in New York, and it is because of the fact that at Los Angeles it is always a question of making a picture 125 miles away from the studio that the cost is increased.

Of course, this letter is not being written because of Edwards and Farnum. After all, that is a settled question. I refer to directors you have there who might have that great desire to go away on vacations for indefinite periods and run up this tremendous cost.

The figures originally submitted on *The Last of the Duanes* were incorrect. The correct figures are $58,037.83 without Farnum's salary.

Very truly yours,
(signed) William Fox

New York City
February 13, 1920

Mr. S.M. Wurtzel
Los Angeles

My dear Sol:

Replying to your telegram which reads as follows: "Daredevil Aviator Ormun Locklear who was featured in Universal picture the *Great Air Robbery* is available stop Locklear has reputation of being greatest air devil wonderful stunt man with airplane automobile motorcycle is also wonderful stunt man in line of work done by Fairbanks and George Walsh stop I reviewed Universal picture Great Air Robbery and if Locklear had good story with things he is capable of doing this picture would have been sensational. stop believe that with good vehicle sensational production could be made with Locklear which could be exploited on big basis stop if you are interested please wire and I will get full particulars on Locklear as to salary et cetera."

I do not see how Fox Film Corporation can be interested in the services of this man. If at this time you were contemplating doing a picture and had a scenario prepared and approved by me, that Fox Film would be willing to exploit as a special production, and this particular story had in it stunts of the kind that Locklear can do, then of course it would be a different proposition. Without having the vehicle of the type and kind necessary in connection with a special production, I cannot see on what basis we can possible be interested in his services.

The great progress and stride that the picture business has made warrants that a 20th century film company have each year a certain number of extraordinary pictures of the type and kind that can be sold to the exhibitor without having a star. The kind I have reference to are the four which were made by the Universal Company; one called *The Beast of Berlin*, second, *Heart of Humanity*, third, *Right to Happiness* and fourth, *Blind Husbands*. Each one of these four special pictures were made by the Universal Company to sell to all high class theaters. The four pictures are pictures of merit and neither one of them depended on a star. But it had for its theme a subject that was being discussed worldwide and therefore, lent itself to special production.

I have in work at present two productions of the type that Fox Film hopes to make special productions of to be ready for release in September. The kind of pictures I have in mind are not easily obtained and when they are obtained, do not depend upon large expenditures in the making of same. The picture itself is to depend on an idea that it contains and second, in the quality of direction.

Realizing that you have a great deal more work than you possibly can attend to I have never invited you to participate in this branch of business because the making of one of these pictures without a star, I find occupies more time than the making of pictures with stars, for when a picture is made in which a star is featured, he or she is supposed to carry the story even if the story has little or no merit; especially in view of the fact that an exhibitor has no alternative and must play it, good or bad.

In a special picture without a star, there the entire thing depends upon the quality of the story and the craftsmanship of the director; and the many days and weeks, and sometimes months that are spent first in the selection of the story, second in the proper preparation of the story; and the company which is fortunate enough to pick a right story and properly prepare it, can ultimately finish that production without much cost and usually results in benefit to the corporation.

If in the future you find such a vehicle, send me a copy of the story in great detail and a letter at great length reciting just what you depend on and how you reached the conclusion that that story will make an exceptional story without a star, and if my ideas concur with yours and if in that story there is a part which Locklear can play, then of course we will be interested in his services, and not otherwise.

You are invited to be on the lookout for material that will make an extraordinary special production. Fox Film Corporation up to this time has made very few of them. In fact, it has failed in most instances where it attempted to do so. I will try to enumerate the special productions we made without stars as follows:

1. *The Honor System*; We succeeded with that.

2. *Cheating the Public*; While it was a good picture when originally planned, it was a financial failure because the time which this play was a propaganda for passed and the public were no longer underpaid and therefore not interested in the subject.

3. *Jack and the Beanstalk*; This was successful. However, in carrying out this idea of fairytales, the net result of the combined fairytales gave the company a loss. The company should have made a handsome profit if it had stopped at the conclusion of Jack and the Beanstalk, but it ruined its chances by insisting on a series of these fairytales.

4. *Woman and the Law*; Which was based on the La Salle case, proved a financial failure.

5. *Blindness of Divorce* made by Lloyd, a financial failure even though a slight profit is shown on this production. However, it is not of the kind of profit I have in mind for an extraordinary picture and was not the type of story that would create a sensation when exhibited. It was just an ordinary motion picture.

6. *The Caillaux Case*: Was not a financial success because it was based on notoriety at a time when the public had war troubles of their own and were not interested in Mr. Caillaux.

7. *The Prussian Cur*: A rank failure.

8. *Why America Will Win*: A rank failure. Both failures caused by the signing of the Armistice. Both of these were war pictures and of course, ended and died with the signing of the armistice.

9. *Why I Would Not Marry*: Everyone at the Home Office thought we had a picture of exceptional merit — failure.

10. *Every Mother's Son*: A propaganda picture that died with the Armistice.

11. *Checkers*: A financial success.

This includes the entire endeavor of the Fox Film Corporation from the inception of special productions without stars. You will note from the above only two of these were successful; *The Honor System** and *Checkers*.† *Checkers* of course you know was a play of world renown. It had been on the stage for 25 years and was printed in book form and millions of copies sold.

From the above analysis you can readily understand the great difficulty there is in soliciting a story for special production without a star, and the necessity of the careful selection of the vehicle before the exhibitor and public will accept a story without a star to the extent of making it a financial success. I say financial success because the greater portion of pictures made by Raoul Walsh were artistic successes, but when he left the employ of the company, our books showed that during the 4½ years that he was with us, we have lost money. The last special production we made with him was the Clemenceau story *The Strongest*. This contained an idea and vehicle that should have made a stupendous picture and should have created a sensation. Raoul Walsh as usual, failed, and therefore it will be classed with the failures of special productions that he made.

To make pictures without stars of the type and kind that I want the Fox Film Corporation to make at least six a year, is more easily said than done and it is because of this I have invited you into the participation of selecting a story for Fox Film Corporation in which no stars should appear.

The only company that I know of that has successfully done this is the Universal. They evidently have some one in their scenario department who has a creative brain and who watches for all timely subjects and manages to hit the nail on the head oftener than all the other companies combined. They bend their entire force and strength to the occasional special production which they have learned is the product which earns the greatest profit.

*Based on prison reform. †Written by Henry Blossom.

All this is sent you for your information. I do not want you to neglect any portion of your business in the search for this material. I, who have been searching in New York for the past year, know how difficult it is to find a proper story that will make a real, successful special production.

The following facts should be interesting to you: For the *Honor System* we paid $250 and it contained an idea that made it possible to rent to a half million dollars.

For *Checkers* we paid $3,000 and it contained an idea and a play that enabled us to rent that picture to a half million dollars or more.

You were at Los Angeles when Lloyd attempted *The Blindness of Divorce.* I had written you about the matter at great length telling you what kind of propaganda was wanted in connection with this picture. You and Lloyd both disregarded my warning. That story was possible if someone with real brains had been engaged to work out the great problem and the trials and tribulations caused by *The Blindness of Divorce.*

One thing is sure — that when the vehicle is found that it requires a director of exceptional merit to put it over. The Universal is blessed with two such directors in its employment.

J. Gordon Edwards intends to make a special production without a star at the conclusion of Farnum's present contract before he starts on his new contract. As you know, it is *The Queen of Sheba.* Of course, that will not be a propaganda picture but rather an exceptionally intense dramatic spectacle. It is to be of the type and kind of story as *Salome* and *Cleopatra.* Both *Salome* and *Cleopatra* could have been made without stars and would have been successful — more successful than they were with the stars.

You caused this letter to be written by the telegram quoted above. Use this information to your best advantage. It would indeed be a great pleasure for me to compliment you on a special production without a star that can prove a financial success for the Fox Film Corporation.

> Yours very truly,
> (signed) William Fox

> New York City
> March 1, 1920

Mr. S.M. Wurtzel
Los Angeles

My dear Sol:

In reply to your letter #3, I note your comment with reference to the Farnum Company. Surely you knew that the rainy season was on when

Edwards arrived. Why didn't you persuade him to abandon the exterior scenes and do the interior scenes first?

Tom Mix: I note what you say and have no comment to make.

William Russell: I note what you say and have no comment to make.

Madelaine Traverse: I note what you say and have no comment to make.

Buck Jones: I note what you say and have no comment to make.

Shirley Mason: I have written you in another letter with reference to *Molly And I* and with reference to the next story for Miss Mason.

I have noticed your comment on the Sunshine Comedy situation. Also that portion with reference to shipping a comedy every week which is satisfactory to me. You also say that the larger comedy is nearing completion and you *think* it will be finished within the $115,000 mark. There should be no thinking about it. I did not authorize the expenditure of another dollar beyond $115,000. It was only thru pressure upon the Board of Directors that I was able to get the additional $15,000 and it was with my positive promise that the picture would not exceed $115,000.

In view of the fact that you are making changes in *The Iron Heart*, it is necessary that you will have *The Spirit of Good* in New York not later than March 26th. That will give me time to review it, have it retitled, printed and shipped to the various offices for release on April 18th. Guide yourself accordingly.

I note your comments with reference to the special productions, *Shuffle and Deal* and *My Husband's Wives*. When these stories arrive I will give them my personal attention and advise you whether I think they possess the kind of material for Special Productions.

Mr. Zanft* has returned and he told me of the very courteous treatment you extended him and he has reported many complimentary things about you. Of course, he is of the opinion that there is too much work put on your shoulders and while you work day and night, he feels it is hardly possible for you to give the various departments the kind of attention they require. I fully realize that from time to time your work has been enlarged to the maximum extent. I hope to relieve you just as soon as we are completely set here in New York.

It is because of the above condition that I am afraid a great deal of waste now exists on the coast; because of your inability to give the kind and type of attention that the plant requires so that it will work more economically and in a more efficient way. If such is the case and if you agree that the work has gone beyond you, I wish you would write me. Such a confession on your part would not detract from your value, but rather

John Zanft — General Representative of Corp.

compel me to reinforce you with executives so that the greatest efficiency can be accomplished and so that in future productions, there will be greater merit than in the past, which will be necessary to meet the great competition that will confront us at the beginning of next season.

> With kindest regards,
> Yours very truly,
> William Fox

New York City
March 3, 1920

Mr. S.M. Wurtzel
Los Angeles

My dear Sol:

I have your letter of the 25th. I have covered most of it in my previous letter to you, which you must have by this time.

With reference to your paragraph commencing as follows: "My experience has been that directors as far as possible try to avoid the making of night scenes, etc.," I disagree with you from actual experience here in New York. I find that directors like to arrange their scenarios to photograph at night. They consider it artistic and they therefore desire to do it that way. I would discourage them if I were you as much as possible. It means nothing to the general public.

I have reviewed *One Quarter Apache*. There is no doubt in my mind that this picture will be accepted and rank amongst the best Tom Mix pictures that we have made. It is will however need careful editing and cutting in order to eradicate most of the bad acting it contains.

In your last letter you called attention to the fact that there are many spots in the picture where the direction is amateurish, and not up to our standard. You are right about that. Mix's acting performance is the worst I have ever seen him give. It is very evident that Jaccard (Jacques) knows how to create action in a picture, but he knows nothing about directing dramatic sequences. Either that or Mix directed himself in his own dramatic scenes. The cost of this picture from the present figures that we have before us is $73,000. As to how much more it will be depends upon what unpaid bills you have. Of course in my opinion this is just willful waste. As I have written you in one of my previous letters, Mix is of the opinion that for a picture to be interesting and worth while there must be large crowds of people employed therein. I particularly call your attention to the scenes in which in the second episode of Mix's character where they elect him sheriff, it would be just as impressive to have stated on the screen that the populace have elected him for sheriff. Instead of which they have several hundred people greeting and yelling all of which does not add to the dramatic quality of the picture except to satisfy and appease Mix's personal vanity.

I do not know how long it took to photograph this scene, or how much it cost to construct, or what the salaries were of these people. But whatever it was, it was an absolute waste. This of course cannot be avoided by me at this end, and can only be avoided by you when the original scenario is written. It must have been clear to you that this incident in the picture would have no dramatic quality and would not help the production; and the money expended on it as waste.

The lavishness and expenditures in this picture gives evidence that Jaccard, having freed himself from the bondage of the Universal Company, made up his mind that he was going to surpass scenically and by mobs, anything that Griffith had ever done. He probably felt that it was his big chance and he was going to take advantage of it at the expense of the Fox Film Corporation. If the story that he is now doing requires dramatic direction of the type and kind that appeared in *The Feud* you may rest assured that the second picture is going to be of no value, for this man I am sure cannot make any character give a dramatic performance. In view of this, he is not to be considered for *The Untamed*.

Were it not for the excess cost and squander that is evident in this picture, I would be more than delighted with the production in spite of the fact that Jaccard failed to have his characters give intense dramatic performances.

In the last paragraph of your letter, you try to justify the reason why you wired for $60,000. You say that the actors payroll went down although the amount was increased because of the Edwards and LeSaint Companies being on location. However, upon examination, I find that Bills Payable have increased from $42,000 to $49,000. Therefore, your total for that week was $67,000 rather than $60,000. This is far in excess of what we have contemplated expending on the coast for work that is being done there, and I am wondering whether or not it would be a good thing to again send someone to the coast in order to reorganize conditions so that the eliminations can be made from our payroll. This becomes necessary ever so often. We are just going thru that kind of a period in New York. In moving into our new building we are reorganizing every department. We are chopping from our payroll thousands and thousands of dollars per week, and have greater efficiency than we did when we had an excessive amount of help.

I am wondering whether a similar condition does not exist at the coast; whether you are not overburdened and top-heavy in every department and whether it would not be advisable to have somebody from New York to reorganize conditions so that we can get back to earth.

I wired you this week telling you that no greater amount than $45,000 could be sent to you each week. I expect $45,000 to be a sufficient amount to carry on the Los Angeles plant. Therefore, you can see the necessity of your withdrawing from the plant for a day or so and make a complete survey of the whole thing. In the future, I will be unable to send you more than $45,000 in any one week.

Very truly yours,
William Fox

New York City
March 8, 1920

Mr. S.M. Wurtzel
Los Angeles

My dear Sol:

I have your weekly letter #4 dated February 29th. Your first paragraph is damn unsatisfactory. I consider it a rather impertinent statement for the beginning of a letter. You are expected to make a prediction with reference to the quality of a motion picture before you start it and likewise are expected to estimate its cost before you start it. I never assumed that when you left my office to take charge of the Coast Studios, that it was possible for you to assume the arrogance indicated in the first paragraph of your letter. I would much prefer to believe that this was written other than intended. Has opportunity sought by every individual which kind fortune was good enough to execute for you made you forget the long, tiresome hours here in New York? It is possible that you as an individual have grown bigger than your position?

Do I understand from your letter that your idea is in the future to go ahead and make productions without being responsible for them as to the cost or quality? If it is bad, it is bad — and if it is good, then it is good? I am mighty sure that you did not intend to write this paragraph. In fact, it is hardly the result of your brain. In your next letter please withdraw that paragraph and continue to make predictions in your weekly reports and estimate the cost of the pictures and the length of time it will take to photograph them.

I do not expect this correspondence between us to be of a nature of a battle of wits. I assume you are capable of carrying out the terms of my letter.

With reference to *Three Gold Coins*, I note that you say that after reviewing the picture you will then compare it with the synopsis sent to you by Miss Baker and that you will take your most competent staff to review this film and then will lay out a plan for rephotographing to make this picture possible for release. That is not satisfactory. The statement "possible for release" means nothing to the Fox Film Corporation, but I do not intend to release any pictures with Mix unless they are really worth while productions. However, after you have reviewed this picture with the competent staff that you refer to, and then after they have rewritten it, I note that you intend to send me the synopsis. I want to receive this before you intend to photograph these scenes, with an estimate of what it will cost to do this additional work, as outlined in your proposed plan, so that I might reach the conclusion first as to whether the production will be of the type and kind that we will want to make with Mix, and whether the cost will be within our reach. I may determine to destroy the present negative and not bother about fixing it up at all.

Your third paragraph contains misleading statements. They are incorrect. The increased funds that you are asking us to send are caused by the excess cost on each picture that you have shipped in the last three months. When Reynolds directed Mix, forty or forty-five thousand was considered excessive by you, and in fact while I was in Europe, because he spent forty-nine thousand dollars, you discharged him. Today, according to the sheet enclosed, you will find that you are spending without much thought, sixty, seventy, seventy-five thousand dollars. If you want to know where this extra money is going, why don't you sit down and look over your statements of a year ago, and this year, and find your comparison.

Before Russell (William) came with the Fox Film Corporation, Russell never in his life posed in a picture that cost, including his salary and other expenses, more than twenty thousand dollars. In fact, twenty thousand was considered exorbitant. The best pictures that were made with Russell and which prompted me to engage him, cost twelve, fourteen and fifteen thousand dollars respectively. Answer me then why, working for the Fox Film Corporation, you, the man in whom I have placed every confidence and one whom I thought sufficiently of to go the coast and try to relieve my mind, are permitting according to the attached report expenditures of fifty and sixty thousand dollars. If you want to know the reason why the New York office breaks its back every Monday morning to get you the transfers that your request, look at the attached and I ask you whether you think it is fair for you to permit this squandering of money such as being spent on these productions.

I refer you specifically to a letter which you addressed to me a year ago asking me to please send you more companies because you could handle them and thereby cut down the overhead charged to each company. I complied with your request but failed to find the result. I am more than certain that if you were the same boy that you were when you sat along side of me for about two years, and if you still have the aggressiveness that you possessed at that time — if you are the same Sol, that I bid good-bye to take care of my picture plant in Los Angeles, if time has not changed your demeanor and if you are still alive to the absolute necessity of making pictures within a stipulated cost, then you would by all means sit down immediately and start to analyze the cost this year as compared with last and I am sure that if you are all that I thought you were, you will necessarily be prompted to sit down immediately and write me a letter stating that these matters are going to receive your prompt attention, the same way as you took care of them when you first arrived in Los Angeles. I am sure that after you have studied the situation, you are going to find that you can produce these pictures within a satisfactory cost; I am sure that you are going to find out that there will be no necessity for the request of excessive transfers; I am sure you are going to find that because of the lesser amounts wired to you on Mondays, at your request, while not increasing the bills payable, I am sure you are going to find that you can master the situation so that it will reflect creditably upon you.

However, I am awaiting eagerly and anxiously for a reply which must necessarily let me know whether you are still the keen and alert person you were in the past when you were in New York or whether the position has become too much for you to handle.

With reference to Edwards and the Farnum company, I am indeed sorry that his company ran into the rainy season and was delayed. Because of it, however, I suppose Edwards will make up for the lost time on his second picture, so that you will be able to strike a fair average as to the cost of both at the completion of the second picture.

I have asked Mr. Leo to ship you *Merely Mary Ann*. We have had many inquiries to sell our rights for this play. This is of course the play that made Marguerite Clark famous on the dramatic stage. It is by Israel Zangwill. I have also asked Mr. Leo to send you the scenario from which this picture was made and to send you the original manuscript of the play. This is a play as though it were written and made to order for Shirley Mason. If you do not decide upon the Japanese play, and if you do not find another vehicle to take its place, then you may prepare for the next story *Merely Mary Ann*.

Instruct your Publicity Department not to do any corresponding with the home office in connection with *Merely Mary Ann* for we are now trying to purchase from the company the complete rights for this play. Previously we produced this picture on a royalty basis.

I will wire you just as soon as this transaction is consummated, at which time you will then be able to remove the restriction on the Publicity Department from withholding any news on this story.

Yours very truly,
(signed) William Fox

Director	Title		Actual Cost	Approximate Maximum Cost
LeSaint	#15	*The Feud*	$69,754.66	$40,000
Mitchell	# 4	*Tricksters 3*	$22,003.09	$20,000
Dunlap	# 6	*Hell Ship*	$25,219.37	$20,000
Beal	# 7	*Flash & Pan Man*	$17,479.37	(better than estimate)
Swickard	# 1	*The Square Shooter*	$24,512.97	$20,000
Smith	# 1	*The Cyclone*	$56,885.31	$40,000
Mitchell	# 5	*Black Shadows*	$24,585.23	$20,000
LeSaint	#16	*Flames of Flesh*	$34,098.35	$30,000
Laurence	#11	*What Would You Do*	$30,116.30	$20,000
Smith	#23	*Gold Coins*	$39,706.21	O.K.
Dunlap	# 7	*The Elephant Man*	$33,007.56	$30,000
Flynn	# 2	*Lincoln Highway Man*	$49,228.03	$35,000
Clift	# 1	*The Last Straw*	$31,000.87	$20,000
LeSaint	#17	*White Lies*	$27,929.64	O.K.
Mitchell	# 6	*The Penalty*	$25,896.12	$20,000
Flynn	# 3	*Shod with Fire*	$59,722.32	$35,000
Mitchell	# 7	*Molly & I*	$30,302.32	O.K.
LeSaint	#18	*Mother of His Children*	$34,113.84	$30,000
Jaccard	# 1	*One Quarter Apache*	$74,163.03	$40,000
Clift	# 2	*Iron Heart*	$25,959.30	$20,000

Los Angeles
March 9, 1920

(Copy)
Mr. William Fox
New York City

My dear Mr. Fox:

I wish to acknowledge your letter of March 1st, which is in reply to my weekly letter number 3.

With reference to the Traverse picture, *The Spirit of Good*, I will do my best to ship the picture to you by March 26th.

I note what you say about the picture *The Iron Heart*. The only reason I did not dismiss Denison Clift for falling down on the picture was because he would be still be of great value to us in the Scenario Department, where he was originally. We need him there because of the fact that we are short of competent people in that department.

With reference to director Lynn Reynolds, I have entirely forgotten my personal feeling regarding him, and if his coming back to the Fox Film Corporation to direct Buck Jones would be beneficial to the Fox Film Corporation,

I would be more than pleased to have him come back. I will get in touch with him immediately and find out whether he is available, although I am still of the firm opinion that if I were permitted to handle Buck Jones and use my judgment as I see best, I will make him a big asset to the Fox Film Corporation.

I wish you to bear in mind that Mix still has in mind that Buck Jones is working here. Anything I do regarding the making of Buck Jones pictures must be done by me in a very diplomatic way without exciting Mix's animosity. Three weeks ago Mix came into my office and asked me if we would continue to make pictures with Buck Jones. I evaded the question. Mix said that it was up to him to protect himself and protect his future. Without explaining what was on his mind, he of course meant that the continuing of making Buck Jones pictures was in opposition to him, and that he would throw every obstacle in the way of making successful Buck Jones pictures.

Tom Mix knows that Lynn Reynolds made good pictures with him; he would also know that if we engaged Reynolds to make pictures with Buck Jones just what that would mean, and would result in a great deal of antagonism similar to the kind we have had with him in the past six months. I have Mix now in a position where he is acting as he used to act two years ago. If Mix wants to work with his heart and soul, he will not only make better pictures, but make them far more economical. But with a spirit of intense animosity, we will get just the opposite results. We had an example of this when we made the picture, *The Feud*.

I know that Mix is under a strict and firm contract with Fox Film Corporation, but there is no doubt in my mind that you know that when a star does not want to work with a firm, it would be very costly. Therefore, the situation has to be handled in a very delicate way, and I must try to get good results with Buck Jones without exciting Mix's suspicion that we are engaging special directors in order to make very good pictures with Buck Jones.

However, I will get in touch with Lynn Reynolds, and if he wants to come with us, I will re-engage him. However, I will wire you first before making final arrangements with him.

I am pleased to note that you liked the picture, *Molly and I*.

I note what you say with reference to the story *His Harvest*. In looking up my records, I find that I have not sent you a copy of the scenario, and I am, therefore, enclosing you a copy herewith. We have had to make a great many changes from original book, which I think were made for the best.

I was pleased with the paragraph in your letter about Mr. Zanft. It gave me great pleasure to be courteous and of help to Mr. Zanft.

With reference to that portion of your letter of March first which refers to my being burdened with work, and that you do not know whether it would be advisable to have some one from New York come out here to look over the business and of the situation with a view of trying to economize and decrease the cost of the pictures. I have given this matter very careful attention.

I realize the fact that during the two and one half years that I have been here, in which time you have never sent anyone from the New York office to look over and check up the business end of the Studios, with the exception of the two months that Mr. Kingston was here, shows to me better than anything of the faith that you have in me. However, I know that no matter what reasons I may give to you as to why a picture made in the Los Angeles Studios cost more than the sum allotted to it, figures always show; and that excuses mean nothing if the pictures cost so much money that Fox Film Corporation is unable to realize a profit.

During the course of the year we did have pictures that are far below standard and sometimes have to be revised and additional photographing done on them to make possible for release, still as you stated in one of your letters to me, it is not always possible to make a 100 percent picture. This is the experience of every studio.

After giving the subject of the cost very careful thought, my firm opinion is that consistent with the average quality of the productions we are making with the various stars, the average cost of the pictures can be made no less. I believe that I have given the business end of the studio as careful watching and supervision as is possible to be given, notwithstanding the fact of the large amount of other work I have with reference to the scenarios and the productions. However, it is entirely possible that my supervision of the business and of the productions may not be correct, and that if you send some one from New York to supervise it we may show much better results, especially as you say the productions in New York do not cost over the sum allotted to them, and in many instances cost less. The only way of finding out whether this is correct is by sending some one out here to do this.

I, therefore, heartily suggest that you send some one from New York as soon as possible to supervise the business end of feature production and of the comedy productions, and do whatever other work you may require of him.

In going over the work that I have accomplished during the time I have been here, and the work I am trying to accomplish, I find that during the past six months I am devoting more and more of my time to the actual production of pictures. That is to say, in the supervision of the construction of stories and scenarios; the supervising of the production as it is being made, watching every day's work, and if it is unsatisfactory, having the director remake it according to my ideas; taking charge of the actual cutting and editing of the finished production. This work has kept me busy from twelve to fourteen hours a day, and notwithstanding the fact that some of the productions we made during the past six months have not been up to the mark, still I think that in going over the pictures made in Los Angeles, you will find that they show good improvement. I will except only two pictures and those were the Mix pictures, *The Cyclone* and *3 Gold Coins*, and as you already know, they were practically taken out of my hands while Mr. Sheehan was here, and due to Mix's unwillingness to work in co-operation with me. However, that situation is now past history.

Every scenario before the director begins work on it, is carefully read and gone over and changes made in accordance with my ideas and the ideas of the director and scenario writer. The photographing of all scenes every day must have my approval before it passes into the hands of the cutter; and then after the film is put together and cut, it any of the sequences are not what I want them to be, they are remade. This is the reason why I did not ship the Traverse picture, *The Iron Heart* to New York.

Therefore, in view of the paragraphs I have written above, that you send some one from New York to take care of the business end, my suggestion would be, if it meets with your approval, that the man you send to the Los Angeles Studios be here permanently and take charge of all the business transactions, of the business departments, even to the signing of checks, if you wish it; and that this man's word in the studio with reference to the expenditure of money of the Fox Film Corporation be law.

And if it meets with your approval, that I be permitted to devote all of my time to the production of pictures; take entire charge of the scenario department; supervise the photographing of the pictures; cutting and editing of the films, and the business end of the studio be taken out of my hands entirely. In other words, that I be absolutely responsible for the quality of the pictures, and that the business man you have here be responsible for the cost of the pictures. Of course he and I will have to work in complete harmony and co-operation in order to achieve the results that you hope for. I firmly believe that if this suggestion be approved by you, that my value to you will be increased one hundred percent.

In making the above suggestion that the business end be taken out of my hands, I do not in any way mean to infer that I have been licked with reference to the cost of pictures. Every man with a position and responsibility such as mine believes that what he does is right; many times he is wrong, and as I stated above, I know I have been wrong in many instances; that my judgment has not always been correct with regard to certain matters; and I have more than worked to do everything that is possible to help in making better quality of pictures and decreasing the cost.

During all the time I have been here, I have never sacrificed any personal desires to the detriment of the interests of the company, which has always been foremost and uppermost in my mind, and I would be the last one to stand in the way of improving conditions, if they can be improved. Any man that you send out here would have my heartiest co-operation.

Very often when people come out from the New York Offices to visit the studios either for business reasons or otherwise, they seem to be under the impression when they arrive that I resent their coming out. However, after they are here for a few days they always change their minds, for I always view this in the broadest spirit, and I know that when you send people out here you send them out for the benefit of the company and for the benefit of the Los Angeles Studios.

I have never yet written you giving my ideas with reference to the policy of the pictures that we are making. I very often felt, in view of the number of productions that are being made in the Los Angeles Studios now, that I should give you my ideas even though you have never requested me to. I have always made it an important point to keep in close and careful touch with productions that are being made by competitors that are in the class with productions being made by us. I touch on this subject with a view to the cost of the pictures.

It is my opinion that the Excel pictures made with Buck Jones, Madelaine Traverse and Vivian Rich cannot be made for less than $25,000. Occasionally we might be able to make several pictures that will cost less, but these are exceptions. I am referring to the pictures that are being made in Los Angeles Studios; they may be made much cheaper in New York.

I do not think that the Victory pictures that we make with Gladys Brockwell, Shirley Mason and William Russell can be made for less than thirty or thirty-two thousand dollars. Occasionally we may be able to make several pictures between twenty-five and thirty thousand dollars. Russell pictures particularly I do not think can be made in Los Angeles for less than thirty-five thousand dollars. The three pictures that Russell has already made here have all cost more than $35,000.

The Mix picture will cost between fifty and sixty thousand dollars, unless we want to greatly cheapen the quality of the production.

With reference to the pictures made with Farnum, of course everything that I have stated in the previous portion of my letter regarding supervision of production, does not refer to Farnum, for Edwards has entire charge of that, likewise his method in making Farnum pictures controls the cost. A long time ago, when the Fox Film Corporation began releasing their pictures on the Excel and Victory programs, you wrote me a long letter explaining to me the reasons why you elevated the Excel and Victory brand; that you hoped to develop the stars on the Excel brand and put them on the Victory brand; and then take the stars in the Victory brand and develop them and try to put them on a Special basis the same as Farnum and Mix.

Therefore, in the making of pictures with the stars in the Victory and Excel class, I have always kept this in mind. I have always felt that if after making six pictures with an Excel star and there is no hope of advancing him any further; if the cost of these Excel pictures are such that the Fox Film Corporation is unable to realize a profit, would it not be better to drop him? Likewise with the stars in the Victory class.

It seems to me that after a year's product consisting of seven or eight pictures made with a star, we can then be able to tell. To give you a concrete example of what I mean; Shirley Mason's first picture put her in the Victory class immediately. No doubt a lot of this was due to her own personality, although the picture being a good picture, was not an exceptionally great picture.

Buck Jones has not as yet had a chance to show what he can do, having had only one picture released.

Traverse has already been on the Excel program for about a year and a half. It seems to me that in this time Traverse had an opportunity to show whether she could be advanced. Of course I know nothing about how the pictures of the various stars sell, except what I get from hearsay. Would it not be better to drop Miss Traverse, devote the time and energy and money we are spending on her and put it into the Mason pictures, or get someone else instead of Miss Traverse who might show better possibilities?

In stating the above, I do not in any way want you to feel that I am trying to dictate any policy to be pursued, for that is a matter that is in no way my concern. However, I have been thinking about this matter for a long time and I felt that I owe it to you to state my beliefs so that you can take them for what they are worth. It seems a pity to me that we have to devote our energies to some people whom we know may not be of any bigger asset to the company and thereby prevent others who have great possibilities and keep them back from future success.

It is my opinion that the day when one man will have the sole supervision of a great many companies will soon be past. Competition today is becoming keener and keener. People are being brought into motion picture business by studios [and] are being paid tremendous salaries in order to make productions bigger and better. Some have met with good success and some have not. People who a few years ago would have laughed at the idea of devoting their time and energy and brains to the motion picture business, by that I mean writers of plays and books, are today coming into the picture business. I refer to Goldwyn and Metro Studios particularly.

I believe that in the future the best results will be obtained by having one competent man supervise the production of four companies, these four companies to be under his sole supervision and control; and that another competent man have control of four other companies. I do not believe the best results can be obtained by having one man take charge of six or seven or eight companies and keep these companies working all the time with very little lay-off, and keep the production cost down.

Good scenario writers, good directors, good cameramen, in fact everything entering into the production of pictures, including artists, are getting to be more difficult. The salaries these people receive in comparison to what they got two and three years ago, is enormous. Naturally the companies who are releasing all their productions on the Special basis instead of program basis, and who are willing to pay more for their actors and directors and writers, are getting the cream of the market. This is what Goldwyn and Metro are doing. Lasky company carry tremendous list of stock actors and actresses. These same faces are seen in almost every one of their pictures. Personally, I do not think this is a good policy; we should see different faces in every picture.

Universal Film Company make two classes of productions; one class on the program basis and the other class, the big productions that are being made by Von Stroheim (Eric), Allan Holubar* and the pictures they are putting out with Priscilla Dean. The cost of some of these pictures; *Blind Husbands* was about $180,000. Von Stroheim was on this picture about six or seven months. *The Right to Happiness* cost almost the same sum of money. Universal has just finished a picture with Priscilla Dean called *The Virgin of Stamboul* which they worked on for six months and which cost $200,000. These figures are not theoretical, but actual, for I have kept a careful watch on their production and on the length of time they have been on them.

By this I do not mean that the productions should cost that much money. They could be made for much less with the same results.

I have written all of the above after careful consideration and review of the entire situation, which I feel would be to the best interests of the Fox Film Corporation.

If you wish, I will be more than glad to write you from time to time giving you my impression and my ideas of thing that I see going around me all the time, and suggestions and comment that I think might be of value or aid to you, similar to the above suggestions that I have made in some of my previous paragraphs with reference to productions with various stars.

I will be more than pleased to hear from you with reference to the matters I have spoken about so that I can get an intimate viewpoint of your feelings and advice regarding the matter. I have always felt that a more intimate viewpoint would be of great help, and very often have felt if I could see you personally just for two hours it would be of great help to me.

It is two and one half years since I have seen you and that is a very

Another actor-turned-director.

long time considering the fact that we are thirty five hundred miles apart, and the only way we have been communicating in the past is either thru telegram or letter, or some one coming out from New York. I have never suggested my going to New York to see you for business here has been too big and too important for me to ever leave the studio for more than a day or two at a time. It requires my personal attention almost every minute, and I have sometimes felt during the course of your work you might come to Los Angeles. When I left New York, one of the last things you said to me was that you would be out to Los Angeles in the near future, but I know that is not a very easy thing for you to do.

In view of the fact that I have in this letter possibly expressed what has been in my mind and heart more than I have ever in any previous letter, I felt that two or three hours of personal conversation would be of great benefit, and if your plans are such that you did not anticipate to come to Los Angeles for a very long time, and conditions here will permit, I may be able to get away and come to New York to see you, even if it is only for a day or two. I have never taken into consideration the fact that I have not seen any of my family since I have been out here, because I would never at any time do anything that will interfere with my work at the studios here.

With reference to the first paragraph in your letter of March first with reference to Edwards working on his exteriors during the rain, I beg to say that during his entire picture Edwards had four days interior work; and as to whether he photographed these interiors at the beginning of the picture or the end of the picture, would have made no difference, on account of the weather situation. Edwards was five weeks photographing the picture, and four weeks and two days of this work was exterior work.

With kindest regards, I am
Yours very truly,

Los Angeles
March 9, 1920

(Copy)
Mr. William Fox
New York City

My dear Mr. Fox:

I wish to acknowledge your letter of March 3rd with reference to the production, *One Quarter Apache* or *Desert Love*. The final total cost of this picture was $74,076.

Of course I agree with you with reference to Jaccard, that he did not show in this picture that he is capable of handling dramatic sequences, for I mentioned this fact in my letter to you when I shipped the picture.

In reference to the sequence that you mentioned in your letter, if the mob scene used when Mix was elected Sheriff, I wish to say that we used this mob in two episodes; one when he was elected sheriff, and then when Mix brings the prisoner into town. Both these sequences were photographed in one day. The total cost of the extras used in these two sequences was $750.

I note what you say about being able to eliminate the particular scene where Mix is elected sheriff and to have inserted a title instead. In the sequence before we showed Mix when he was seven years of age and then jumped a space of about twenty years to where he is elected Sheriff. It was a grave question in my mind whether a title explaining Mix being elected Sheriff, in view of the lapse of time, would have been accepted by an audience.

After all, it is a question of the good judgment of a man who goes over the scenario, and in this case, as you say, my judgment was wrong. I do not want you to be under the impression for a moment that I am permitting scenes to be photographed which require large numbers of people and large sets simply because either the star of director or I want to make a very good showing.

I want to call your attention to the fact that the Western street used in this picture was not a set erected by us, but it was a Western street that is owned by the Universal Film Company, which we rented from them for $150 a day. We used this street six days. The hacienda was not erected by us, but was a set owned by the Universal Film Company which we rented for $125 a day and which we used four days. By renting these acts instead of erecting them, we saved approximately five thousand dollars on the technical cost of the production. As it was, the technical cost was high, for in spite of the fact that we rented the Western street and hacienda, we had to do a lot of difficult and trick construction work on the exterior and interior of the mining shaft and some other sets.

In mentioning the above, I am not trying to justify the cost, which I know was more than should be spent for a Mix picture.

Yours very truly,

New York City
March 15, 1920

Mr. S.M. Wurtzel
Los Angeles.

My dear Sol:
I have your letter of the 9th. It was interesting for three reasons; first,

because it was human; secondly because it was constructive and third because it carried a proper tone, so different from the tone of your letter of the 29th.

I agree with you that greater efficiency could be had if there were seven or eight companies working in Los Angeles, to have one man take charge of not more than half the number. With this in mind, as early as possible and it is convenient, I will carry out the thought you suggested. At present, I do not know when I shall be able to come to Los Angeles. I tried my best to do it this last winter, but moving into our new building made it impossible. I will try in the near future to arrange my work so that it will be possible for me to go there. Your coming here at this time before the above change is made, is hardly possible in view of the fact that at this time the Los Angeles Studios are spending at the rate of three million dollars per annum; and that expenditure cannot go on without supervision.

The matter of eliminating such stars as have not advanced, has been a much discussed subject here in New York. At the convention which is to be held early in May of the branch managers, a conclusion will be reached as to which of these should be eliminated and which should be advanced from one program to another. After that I will communicate with you immediately and inform you of the result.

The statements made in your letter are a complete surprise to me. I never knew that you were restraining yourself from writing to me about all things going about you. If you were restraining yourself from making suggestions that would be of help to the Fox Film Corporation, you need not do so any longer. You know that my policy is to receive any sugges-tions from any employee of the company — particularly from you in view of the responsibility that I have entrusted with you. Therefore in the future write me on any subject that you think would be of interest to me or the Fox Film Corporation.

Yours very truly,
William Fox

WESTERN UNION TELEGRAM
(copy)

Los Angeles
March 18, 1920

William Fox
New York City

Acknowledging our letter March eight have carefully noted contests extremely regret my weekly letter number four did not convey that which

I intended stop I stated in first paragraph I would try to make productions as good and economically as possible in accordance with your wishes stop I did not mean by this that I would go ahead and make pictures without trying to keep cost to sum you required and without being responsible for cost and quality stop I wrote you long letter on March ninth which in a way covers majority of paragraphs in your letter I suggested in my letter that if you do not expect to come to Los Angeles in the near future that I go to New York and see you and have talk with you as I believe this vital necessity in view of the recent correspondence stop

Do not want you to feel that I have changed in any way but am still giving the same aggressiveness attention to production as I did when I first came to Los Angeles but you must realize that production situation in Los Angeles has changed during this time which makes it impossible to make productions at cost you want stop have carefully gone over chart of picture costs attached to your letter and make comparisons with pictures made past two years I admit that costs of some of pictures mentioned in statement did not show in production however there are conditions that arise in the making of pictures which creates excessive cost and which you no doubt have encountered in New York studios stop after careful analyzation of cost chart wish to say that I cannot possibly make similar pictures at costs as set by you stop am writing you detailed letter in answer to your letter of March eighth stop

Recent correspondence has left me in nervous condition and has detracted my mind to great extent from work which is very vital at present stop would therefore appreciate telegraphic reply giving me your viewpoint on my letter of March ninth and this telegram

S M Wurtzel

WESTERN UNION TELEGRAM
(Copy)

New York City
March 19, 1920

S M Wurtzel
Los Angeles

    After you read my letter dated March fifteenth you will get therefrom a clear understanding as to what is expected of you

William Fox

New York City

March 23, 1920

Mr. S.M. Wurtzel
Los Angeles

My dear Sol:

With reference to your letter #6 dated March 13th, I have just sent you the following telegram:

"In order to review print and deliver to our exchanges in time for release *The Orphan* should be in New York Saturday March twenty seven stop each day you fail to send it after that will hurt quality of printing on this picture stop wire me immediately earliest date you can possible ship this picture."

By the time you receive this letter, no doubt you will read *The Challenge of the Law*. Please review it immediately and write me whether or not it can be used for Russell, and if not, I want the story returned so I can read it here with the idea of using it for George Walsh. Mr. Edwards has a synopsis and two continuities which were prepared by two different scenario writers. I presume he has turned the whole matter over to you by now.

I have read your comment with reference to Madelaine Traverse. It is agreeable to Fox Film Corporation to cancel her contract. Bearing this in mind, we should have no difficulty in getting her to appear at the studio at a reasonable hour and making her understand that she is expected to carry out your instructions. Just as soon as you propose to her to tear up the contract (which you are authorized to do after you have photographed the scenes necessary for *The Iron Heart*) you will then have no further difficulty; and if perchance she herself decides to cancel the contract, Fox Film Corporation will be just as satisfied.

With reference to Brockwell's next story entitled *The Little Gray Mouse*, I hope that this is a vehicle with great dramatic strength, for pictures with Brockwell without that have no value. From its name it sounds like a farce. Brockwell is "flopping" sure and fast. Unless her pictures have a great dramatic quality, when the present contract expires, Fox Film Corporation will not be interested in renewing it.

Vivian Rich: I reviewed the Vivian Rich picture *Would You Forgive*? and I find it an interesting story and shall make an acceptable picture by the exhibitors. I note that you were obliged to eliminate every close-up because she cannot stand being photographed at close range. That being the case, Fox Film Corporation is not interested in her services. We have enough trouble without making pictures with someone who cannot stand the camera.

I have sent you the following telegram today with reference to Blystone:

"Clyde Cook* leaves here tomorrow arriving Los Angeles Saturday stop by all means disband Vivian Rich co. until you get director without further delay to complete picture Blystone started stop Fox Film Corp. feels reasonably sure Cook will ultimately take Chaplin's place stop that is by far of greater importance than Vivian Rich pictures stop explain my attitude as expressed in my telegram of last Saturday to Blystone and assure him of my profound regard for his ability stop cannot understand why Blystone would not have his hands full making preparations for his next story with Cook so he may be ready to photograph him on his arrival stop my understanding is that would only result in benefit to his first picture with Cook"

If by the time you receive this letter you have not found a director to take Blystone's place, then you can consider this letter as authorization not to work any further on the Rich picture. If you have found another director and he is ready to work immediately on the Rich story and complete the next picture, you are to make no more.

Buck Jones: I note what you say about Buck Jones' picture — that Dunlap (Scott) will start to photograph it. *All speed will be necessary.* However, a damn fine picture will also be necessary, or otherwise, we will find ourselves in a position with Jones of being unable to elevate him from the Excel Brand.

Because of the great length of time that has expired between the time he took ill and the time we started to photograph him, I presume that the scenario was well examined and revised so as to be dead sure that we have a perfectly wonderful picture with him. It is scheduled for release on May 16th. The present congestion of railroads is such that when we ship a film from New York to Denver, it is in transit from two weeks to longer. Therefore, it is necessary to have the picture here for my reviewing, recutting, printing and shipping one month before the release date, and then we are only getting the film to our offices in the United States on the day of release. — So every day after April 16th that the film arrives in New York will effect the quality of our re-editing and the quality of printing or be late at the offices and compel us to disappoint our exhibitors and lose our customers who figure on this film.

I warn you to watch out that in Buck Jones' pictures, there should appear no false, dramatic notes and the scenes that require excellent dramatic work should be well planned and carefully taken so that the dramatic situation with Buck Jones does not become a farce. We have gone thru such an experience with the first Buck Jones picture made by Swickard (Charles), which we returned to you and which we cannot release because of the ridiculous direction and because of the fact the Jones' acting was on

---

Australian-born acrobat and pantomimist who had a great success at the Hippodrome.

a par with a $3.00 a day extra. Of course, it is not Jones' fault — not that I think he is an actor, but it is the fault of the director who should be able to make a $3.00 a day extra act. That is what the word director means on the screen.

Second: The second picture with Jones was *The Last Straw*, started by Swickard whom you dismissed, and then had Dennison Cliff finish it. Under your supervision, Buck Jones gave an intelligent performance in that picture. While in that picture Jones did not act; you and Cliff understood Jones and did not try to make him act, but rather had him express himself on the screen by keeping perfectly still and conveyed the dramatic scenes required by facial expressions. Therefore, there are two distinct ways of handling Jones. If he possess dramatic acting quality, he should be made to give an acting performance. — If he does not possess dramatic qualities to give an acting performance, then the director must be able to restrain him from acting and have him give a suppressed dramatic performance in which he is not required to use his hands and feet but just facial expressions. That is what happened in *The Last Straw*.

With reference to my attitude re Vivian Rich and Blystone. For the past year and a half I presume that you have made every effort to add to the directing force of the comedy department directors who could make comedy pictures for the money we have authorized to spend. I presume you have been unsuccessful in finding a single director; otherwise, I would have heard from you long before this.

Mr. Sheehan, when he was at the coast, likewise tried to find a director but he too, was unable to do so. Blystone in my opinion has exceptional merit and from what Sheehan has told me he is a very high class gentleman. Sheehan's explanation of Blystone to me has cause me to admire Blystone and to look forward to him to relieve me of an emergency in the comedy plant if one ever arises. It is because of this that I would rather abandon the Rich company than take Blystone from the comedy plant and have him make a dramatic picture, for there are two things I have in mind.

1. If he made a dramatic picture and if it were a knock-out, you would not get him back in the comedy plant.

2. If he made a poor picture you would discourage the man's ambition and would lick him when he came back to the comedy lot.

I do not want to test either one of these two things at this time.

When your telegram came Clyde Cook was in the building and he had already arranged to leave Tuesday, March 23rd, arriving in Los Angeles Saturday, March 27. I feel that Clyde Cook will be of great value to the comedy plant as he is a man of extraordinary qualities, and if the picture turns out a hit we can get extraordinary rentals for it and make comedies in which we can star him in addition to the Sunshine Brand, and in that way be in competition with Harold Lloyd and any other comedian who is now featured and sell for high prices.

It would be too bad not to develop this available piece of property. Why take Vivian Rich into consideration who means nothing to Fox Film Corporation. There are hundreds of pictures made by other companies of the same type that we make with Vivian Rich, and go to waste.

If Clyde Cook's first comedy is a sensation, then no time has been wasted in allowing Blystone to remain idle for a week or so to make proper preparations so that he can start to work without having to stop when his troop is around to gather together the gags.

This letter is of a personal nature. There are many paragraphs in it that only you should be familiar with. Therefore, I am sending it to your home for I do not think every employee at your studio should be familiar with the contents of this letter or with any of my future letters, and I have therefore instructed Mr. Dunn* to forward all mail to your home. Of course, there will be certain letters that are not of a personal nature. Those of course should be filed in the office; otherwise I would file them at home.

Very truly yours
William Fox

Los Angeles
April 7, 1920

(Copy)
Mr. William Fox
New York City

My dear Mr. Fox:

I wish to acknowledge your very important letter of March 23d, which I have very carefully read and given great thought.

I have carefully noted all your paragraphs with reference to Blystone, in which of course, I absolutely agree with you. However, as stated in my previous correspondence my only object was to help us out in the emergency, but I see you are correct — that it will be too much of a chance to take with Blystone and that his services are of far greater value if we were not to take a chance in having him make a dramatic picture.

With reference to my having been unable to find another competent comedy director, the reason for this is very simple. I have already explained to you I my previous letters that Hampton DelRuth is a very fine gentleman, but is working solely for the interest of Hampton DelRuth, and it is

---

Henry Dunn — Fox's secretary, and later, brother-in-law.

naturally his ambition to have such control over the comedy organization that should at any time the Fox Film Corporation desire to make a change, they would naturally have a very difficult time in finding a man to take his place and at the same time keep the comedy organization intact. Therefore, it is his policy to advance only those men who, in the case of an emergency like that, would feel themselves bound to DelRuth rather than to the Fox Film Corporation. Therefore, any comedy director whom I would suggest or would want to engage for the Sunshine Comedies, will either be promptly vetoed by DelRuth, or, if permitted to make a picture, DelRuth would surely put everything in his way to make him a failure.

I note the last paragraph of your letter with reference to filing all your letters that are of personal nature at my home, which I will do.

I wish to refer to your letter to me of February 13th with reference to a production with the dare devil aviator Locklear; and also with reference to the matter of special productions, into which you went into greater detail in your letter.

I am enclosing herewith two stories which, in my opinion, have great merit and value to be considered for Special Productions without a star. By a Special Production I mean a production that will cost approximately from sixty to seventy thousand dollars. The value of the production will depend first, upon the story and what it can accomplish; second, upon the direction; third, the cast, fourth, photography; fifth, sets; and last, the production as a whole.

From my observation the productions that are making the biggest success today are not propaganda pictures, but rather pictures of the type Cecil deMille is making, and Von Stroheim is making. *Blind Husband* was not a propaganda picture, nor was Von Stroheim known. In fact, he was almost unheard of except as an actor of character parts. But his story and the production made it a success. DeMille, of course, is well known as a director, in fact I believe almost as well as D.W. Griffith. His productions are not propaganda, they are rather on a certain type of picture that depend, not so much upon the stories, but rather upon the artistic settings, the cast and the manner in which the production is made; and last but not least the titles of the pictures.

The story, *My Husband's Wives* strikes me as being an excellent subject. First, it is a very good title. The title *My Husband's Wives* immediately will attract any audience. The story has a great appeal to women. In brief it is a story of a girl who marries a man who has traveled extensively over the world; has been married four times; once to an English woman, a French woman, a Spanish woman, and a Russian woman, and divorced in every instance; and then meets an American girl whom he loves and marries. The American wife who knows of her husband's past and of his marriages, is anxious to travel and see the world, whereas he wants to settle down and not do any more traveling. He finally takes his wife abroad, and the rest of the story is based on the American wife meeting the different ex-wives of the husband. There is some remarkable drama throughout these episodes. In fact, throughout the entire story. The finish of the story is that of a dream. However, this can be changed by making it a straight dramatic story. It can be made both ways and either finish selected. The finish of the story, showing the suicide of the young woman, in my opinion, if one of the finest things I have read.

As I said above, it will appeal to women. First, those who are not married because they will be anxious to see a story of a man who has had four wives. Second, it will appeal to married women because a situation like that always does appeal to them as something that might have happened in their lives.

The story offers great opportunity for color and for beautiful settings. No exterior sets will have to be built. The whole story can be played in interiors. Any exteriors necessary can be obtained around the studio.

The story *Environment*, although treating of a subject which is not new, and that is of East and West intermingling, still of all the stories I have seen on that subject, this struck me as being positively by far the best. You will note in the story that the author avoids the excessive use of crowds. However, one of the big items of expense would be the building of an Indian setting.

The thing that struck me about this particular story outside of its great dramatic value is the fact that at the present time the eyes of the world are fixed on this question of East and West. Conditions in Europe and Asia are so unsettled, that a story of this kind would be of great interest. It is my opinion that the big political question in the next few years which is fermenting now is the question of England regaining its influence over countries such as India, Canada, Ireland, etc. Therefore, a subject of this kind would be of interest in that respect.

I am sending you these two stories after having given both very careful thought, and putting a great deal of work in them to perfect them, and it is my recommendation that I be permitted to produce these two stories, if they meet with your approval, at the Los Angeles Studios. There is one director whom we have here in whom I have the greatest confidence. I believe he can make these two stories worthy of Special Production — the kind which will be able to earn for the Fox Film Corporation great sums of money. The director I refer to is E.J. LeSaint.

With reference to the aviator Locklear, the reason I have not written you before about this was because at the time received your letter of February 13th, Locklear was not in a position to do any business. However, during the past week I have had several talks with him and he is now available.

It is my opinion that the production of the kind I have in mind for Locklear will be the biggest money-making picture Fox Film Corporation has ever had. This is a rather big statement and covers a large territory, but after seeing this man's work, taking to him personally and knowing what a success his first picture with Universal Film Company was which was a mediocre picture — a high class production, a good story made by a good director, with thrills and stunts that can be injected by Locklear, will make it a most sensational production. It is inconceivable to the ordinary person who has not seen Locklear perform, to know what he can not only do with an airplane, but with an automobile, motorcycle, motorboat and any mechanical contrivance. And a picture that would be made with Locklear would have every possible kind of thing to make stunts with and not only depend on airplanes. Besides this, Locklear is a splendid athlete, and can do physical stunts the same as are done by George Walsh, Tom Mix and Fairbanks.

In your letter of February 13th you stated you did not see how you could be interested in making a picture with Locklear unless we had a story ready which you could approve of. I am so enthusiastic about this proposition that I am having a writer prepare a special story which will be a comedy drama, giving a man like Locklear an opportunity for every conceivable kind of stunt, and a picture that can be made at a cost of between sixty and seventy thousand dollars. I expect to have this story ready in about two weeks, and will then submit it with a recommendation for your approval.

It is my belief that the Fox Film Corporation will be missing a splendid opportunity if we do not make a production with Locklear. Aviation is at present one of the most talked about subjects, and Locklear is a man who has been advertised for a large extent throughout the country in every way. In my talks with Locklear I explained to him that a story would have to be approved of by you before we can do anything further. Naturally the subject of a salary came up. Locklear stated that he would work for the same salary that he received from the Universal and this is $1650. a week. Out of this money Locklear pays two pilots he has, each of whom receive $100. a week; and Locklear also furnishes two airplanes, we to furnish the gasoline and oil to run the planes, which would be very nominal. The rental of one plane per day would be $125., therefore the amount of money that Locklear asks, in my opinion, is very nominal and very considerate.

It is my opinion that if the Fox Film Corporation were next season to follow out the system of the Metro Film Company this year, that is of making only big plays, big books, and making fewer pictures, that is to say six or seven a year, the returns from them would be far greater than the returns of a larger amount of pictures with stories that are not as big and productions that are not as big. The big fault with the Metro Company, from observation of their work in Los Angeles, is that it has taken them from eight to ten weeks to photograph a production. This, of course, is rank extravagance. It is my opinion that were a production made from an original story or from a play or book, from four to five weeks is ample time to photograph and make a big production. The only difference between the cost of a production made from a big play and a production made from an original story would be the difference between the cost of the story and the play. The rest of the production would remain practically the same possibly a slight increase.

With reference to comedies, it is my opinion that we should continue the same policy as during the past year — one 2-reel comedy every two weeks. But in addition thereto, have two 5-reel comedies similar to the one that is now being made. Of the type of two-reel comedies, it is my opinion that the public is getting away from the old slap-stick comedy. I am making this statement from the talks I have had with exhibitors in Los Angeles and San Francisco.

It is almost impossible to get a high class theatre in Los Angeles or San Francisco like Grauman's or The California to play a two-reel slapstick comedy. There has not been a Senet or Sunshine comedy played in these houses for months, and in talking to these exhibitors they tell me the public does not want them. The type of comedy that is now most popular in the west is the Harold Lloyd comedy and it is my opinion that the future comedies should be a cross between the Harold Lloyd comedy and the type we are now making. This matter has been a subject of discussion between DelRuth and myself for some time, and we have both agreed on it.

By a Harold Lloyd type of comedy I mean comedies with a story and with situations, rather than to depend solely on slap-stick gags.

Mr. Edwards and I have been discussing, for some time, a subject which we think is of the greatest importance, especially in view of the fact that Mr. Edwards is shortly to produce *Queen of Sheba*. In the making of *Queen of Sheba*, he will have to erect exterior sets representing ancient Jerusalem and Arabia. These sets will be the largest item of cost in *Queen of Sheba*. We both thought it would be a pity to have to destroy these sets after making *Queen of Sheba* without getting more value of them.

It is our opinion that right now there is a big religious sentiment sweeping over this country, in fact, over the entire world. This is a natural reaction after the war. The most successful pictures made recently are those dealing with subjects touching on religion, but none of them, however, have touched upon the most important religious subject and that is the Bible.

Mr. Edwards tells me there is a company being organized to photograph the Bible, therefore, it seems that this is a good opportunity for the Fox Film Corporation to make two or three special pictures of some of the most famous Biblical subjects such as Joseph and His Brethren, the story of

David, and any other big Biblical stories of which there are an unlimited number.

The reason for taking up this subject is because, if it will meet with your approval to make such subjects, before we begin work on the sets for *Queen of Sheba*, we can have them in mind and set our plans in making the sets accordingly.

It is my opinion that the film companies who have made the biggest success on special productions are those companies who were able to foresee and foretell what the public demanded, and be the first one on the field with it instead of allowing a competitor to come in and then catch up with him; for naturally the public takes to the picture that is first in the field. For instance, it is my opinion that one of the biggest reasons for the success of *The Spy* was not on account of the production, but due to the fact that the *Spy* was the first anti-German propaganda picture. If you recollect, Fox Film Corporation made this picture before the United States entered into the war with Germany. In preparing the subject, instead of using Germany, we used a mythical country, but as the story was being finished, America entered into the War and Fox was the first in field with that kind of subject.

I am enclosing herewith a memorandum with reference to a matter that has been a subject of the Motion Picture Producers Association for the past six months. This is a subject that Mr. W.J. Reynolds, secretary of the association took up with you when he saw you in New York, and that is the organization of a company to be known as the Cinema Furniture and Supply Company with a capital stock of $500,000. of which $150,000. is to be paid in at the organization of the company.

At various meetings held by various studio representatives, it was decided to apportion to the various members of the organization a certain amount of stock to be subscribed by the various companies, according to operation. To the Fox Film Corporation was assigned $10,000.

This organization has not been formed, as it is necessary to obtain the approval of all the studios. I am submitting this memorandum to you for your consideration. The memorandum contains the articles of incorporation of the proposed company together with a statement of its purposes and ideas. Personally, I think the idea is a splendid one, and there is no doubt in my mind that it would prove of great benefit to the motion picture production in Los Angeles. First, because of the fact that it would mean a big savings of money to the studios; second; I am sure it will be a profitable venture; third, the organization of such a company with all the studios behind it, means that it would bring all the studios together into a sort of working organization which would have a good deal of power in the City of Los Angeles.

At the present time all the studios seem to be fighting each other. None of them seem to have a definite object in view; that is, with reference to engaging employees; the buying and renting of furniture and supplies. Business people of Los Angeles charge what they like to each studio. Various studios pay different salaries to different artists. An organization of this kind would mean that the studios would be drawn into more intimate contact with each other, which would necessarily result in greater economy.

I, therefore, suggest that you approve of this organization, and if you do approve of it, to advise me immediately so that I can inform the Motion Picture Producers Association.

I am enclosing herewith a letter written to me by Charles Kenyon, who is now with Goldwyn and who was formerly on our scenario staff. Mr. Kenyon wrote the story entitled *The Devil's Wheel* which we produced with Gladys Brockwell. From the attached letter, Kenyon is of the opinion that the story would make a good stage play, and he would like to make a stage version of it. Will you be good enough to advise me with reference to this matter so that I can reply to Mr. Kenyon's letter.

Yours very truly,
SMW.AS

New York City
April 15, 1920

Mr. S.M. Wurtzel
Los Angeles

My dear Sol:

I have your letter of the 7th.

I note what you say in reference to the comedy situation, treating on Blystone and Del Ruth; I will have it in mind before me at all times. We naturally rely on Blystone in case of an emergency. In the meantime your present attitude towards Blystone is the proper one. Be sure the Clyde Cook comedy is a knockout. There is greater value, in the comedy line, in advancing individual performers, then there is in making a brand of comedies like Keystone and Sunshine that do not draw audiences. It is only the individual performer that creates for himself a following in comedies, that becomes a valuable asset to a company. This is what I hope to accomplish as a result of the Clyde Cook pictures. No doubt you have had this in mind and have explained it to Blystone so that he is working toward that angle.

I note what you say about slapstick comedies not playing the first class theatres in Los Angeles. That is not the case in New York. The Rivoli Theatre here is using Sunshine Comedies and are glad to get them. We have just reissued the first nine comedies, made under the supervision of

Lehrman. These we sold to the Capitol Theatre and they were glad to get them. The first class picture theatres throughout the United States, probably exclusive of Los Angeles, are glad to get consistent comedies. It is true however that they are unwilling to pay fair prices.

That of course is the fault of Mack Sennett and myself. I spoke to his representative the other day, and I explained to him that if his organization and ours worked in harmony, and had a complete understanding with reference to future rental prices, we would soon establish a greater rental. For there is a great demand for first class comedies. The only reason exhibitors are not paying good prices, is because of the competition that exists between Sennett and the Sunshine Brand.

This type of comedy you speak of, such as the Harold Lloyd, depends upon the personality of Lloyd as much as upon the story he appears in. If we depended upon the personality of the comedians in the Sunshine Comedies, the result would be that we would keep the people out of the theatre. During the entire time that Sunshine Comedies were made under the supervision of DelRuth and Lehrman, neither one of the two succeeded in developing a single comedian that became an asset to the company. It might be a good plan to tie a can to them all and start with a new batch, if available. We know the present ones will never make good. It is fair to assume that they all had excellent chances offered to them, if their personalities were of the type and kind the public would accept; but they have no personalities. Half of them are as funny as a crutch. The laughter is caused by the situations and not by their personalities. That is why we have to stick to slapstick and not farce comedies that depend upon the personality of the performer.

Every comedy organization in America is wondering why Harold Lloyd became popular, and why they stood still. We are among those who are wondering. Of course that is not the case with me personally. I realised that Harold Lloyd was becoming popular, and as you know I asked you over a year ago to get in touch with him. Sheehan tried to get him over a year ago. We realised that it was only a question of time when he would be very popular, especially in view of the fact of the absence of Chaplin comedies. In the past year and a half, Chaplin only made three comedies. The reasons why Lloyd became popular are, first, the absence of Chaplin comedies; secondly, because of his personality; thirdly because he has been in comedies a long time and gradually built up a following due to his charming personality.

I have read what you say about Locklear. When the story arrives here, I will read it with much interest and will then give you my decision in the matter.

I have read the several pages with reference to your inquiry of the future policy of the Fox Film Corporation. Also your comment on Special Productions. Also your comment with reference to DeMille.

The policy of the Fox Film Corporation for the next season will be to make a number of pictures, that you mention, per star with the following stars:

William Farnum
Pearl White
Tom Mix
George Walsh
William Russell
Buck Jones
Shirley Mason,

and if we succeed with Eileen Percy, if she has the qualities as described in my previous letter, and if it is possible to make with her pictures of the Constance Talmadge type so that we can continue with her, she will be included in our star series. That makes 8 stars in all and as a result of which we should have between 55 and 65 pictures; plus special productions without stars.

For your information, and that you may be familiar with this thing, this has been planned months ago and is actually being prepared for; the following special productions are either completed, or in work;

Completed: *While New York Sleeps*, in my opinion will be one of the great pictures of the year.

In Work: *My Lady's Dress*, by Edward Knoblock, which I am sure will also be one of the big pictures of the year.

In Work: *The Face at Your Window* by Max Marcin, treating on the great subject that now confronts the country,* and contains the greatest dramatic story I have ever read, and which will also be one of the biggest pictures of the year.

In Work: A story, un-named, teating on the subject that one mother can successfully raise six children, and what a great effort it is for six children to take care of one mother. It is now well advanced and should develop into a wonderful story; the five reel comedy DelRuth made; *The Queen of Sheba* that J. Gordon Edwards is to make. All excepting J. Gordon Edward's story, will be ready to release early in August; and my present plans are to make two or three more extraordinary fine pictures without stars from now to September, and to make them here in New York.

It is not my intention to burden you with greater responsibilities than you now have; but if I were to assign to you the making of special productions, without stars, it would simply mean another source of worry, and

---

Bolshevik propagandists in the United States.

would compel you to devote your exclusive time to such a picture. The result would be that we could be neglecting the other pictures with stars. Because of this, at present it is not my intention to allow any of the pictures without stars to be made in Los Angeles.

Fortunately I am enjoying excellent health at this time, and am ambitious to personally supervise the making of pictures without stars; and because of the excellent studio facilities that we have here in New York, and because of the weather conditions that are before us, and the excellent opportunity for beautiful photography that will exist in New York from now until November, it is my intention to make stories without stars in New York, and not plan to make any in Los Angeles, where the costs of material are at the highest peak. The facilities and possibilities for making special productions in New York are by far of greater advantage than they are in Los Angeles. That is why they will be made here.

It has been firmly in my mind, and I am now convinced more than ever as a result of reading your letter that you do not see LeSaint from a critical standpoint. I am enclosing a cost sheet of four pictures—each one of these four was predicted as being a great dramatic story, and having great dramatic possibilities.

First —*The Flames of the Flesh*—when it arrived here I was keenly disappointed. It did not contain a dramatic quality, but was slow moving, tiresome and dull vehicle.

Second —*White Lies*—a picture we were unable to release up to the present time because of the problems that presented themselves when we reviewed it. We are still trying to edit this picture.

Three —*Mother of His Children*—a meaningless picture.

Four —*Rose of Nome* in my opinion one of the rottenest pictures Fox Film Corporation has ever made. Surely you do not want the man who has failed to make great pictures as described above, to make special productions to cost $70,000 and to rent to $500,000. Evidently you are injected with the germ of director's confidence. Don't you know that Fox Film Corporation never made a picture that rented to that sum of money? Even *The Daughter of the Gods* has still some to go before it reaches that amount. Where did you get those figures from? And why do you listen and let people disturb your peace of mind?

However the rental of a picture should not be a source of worry to you. That is for our sales force. Your worry should be the making of great pictures. If you devote your time in making sure fire Mix, Russell, Buck Jones, Shirley Mason and Eileen Percy pictures, and will make them of a quality that will create for them public recognition, at a fair and reasonable price, you are then doing your work nobly and well.

The two stories you sent are based on the success of an idea created in the mind of Cecil DeMille and is a complete copy of his theory and motive. I am unable to write anything about them at this time. Rest assured that I will read them both carefully and then decide as to whether or not they are material for special production, at which time I will write you again and tell you what my plans are in the matter.

You failed to state the price for these stories. Give me the price the next time you write them. Find out what the author will want for them. In stating the price, kindly enclose me the original letter signed by the author of the stories offering them for sale, stating the price, which I am sure will be reasonable. So if I should decide on one of the two for production, there will be no holding up in this matter later.

I am assuming that these stories have not been submitted to anyone else, and that they have not been peddled in Los Angeles, so that the idea therein contained has not been adopted by someone else. I don't want to find that if I should produce one of these stories, that another producer has embodied the idea in another story.

Of one thing I am certain, that LeSaint has not shown any qualities that would cause me to decide that he is qualified to make special pictures without stars. All of this of course is for your confidential information, and for your guidance and not for discussion with anyone. You are to take no one into your confidence in connection with this letter. Read it and file it in your home and simply use it as reference and guidance.

I carefully noted what you say about sets for *The Queen of Sheba* and of the suggestions by you and Edwards with reference to religious pictures. Pictures of the type of *The Queen of Sheba*, Fox Film Corporation will only make one a year, in line with previous policy, like *A Daughter of the Gods, Cleopatra, Salome*, and *Queen of Sheba*.

In laying out your plans for *The Queen of Sheba*, do not make them with the contemplation of using sets in a religious picture. Dismiss that idea from your mind entirely. Be sure to read this paragraph to J. Gordon Edwards.

I noted our recommendation regarding the Motion Picture Producers Association and have the paper you wish me to sign before me. I don't want Fox Film Corporation to be the leader in this movement. Therefore, the papers will remain on my desk unsigned. If this movement takes foot, and if Artcraft, Goldwyn and other reputable producers of Los Angeles, have entered into it, and a request is made on me by these representatives to join them, then it will receive consideration, and not before.

I read Kenyon's letter to you with reference to the scenario *The Devil's Wheel*. My understanding is that the Fox Film Corporation owns all the rights to this story. If it has great stage possibilities, Fox Film Corporation would be pleased to re-sell the story. If Kenyon is interested in producing it on the stage, let him state a fair price for it in my consideration.

I look forward with great anticipation the receipt of your weekly letters and replying to them. I can readily see the good that is being accomplished by them. I sincerely regret that it was not done from the very beginning, at the time you took charge of the plant. I am sure both you and the Fox Film Corporation would have been materially benefited by the exchange of ideas each week, and by the immediate report of progress made at the studio. For, in the exchange of letters, I get a complete insight of the operation of your mind, just 3,500 miles from New York, and you get a complete insight of the operation of my mind in answering the matters you write about.

I am sure this co-operation will only result in benefit both to yourself and the Fox Film Corporation.

> With kindest regards,
> Yours very truly,
> (signed) William Fox

WESTERN UNION TELEGRAM

> New York City
> April 26, 1920

S M Wurtzel
Los Angeles

Alibis contained in your telegram reference LeSaint's sister to Salome and Brockwell performance are not satisfactory stop however if you want LeSaint to direct Shirley Mason picture and if you think he can make picture within our cost and not in accordance with moneys expended on some of rotten Brockwell pictures then let him proceed.

> William Fox

(Copy)

> Los Angeles
> May 1, 1920

Mr. William Fox
New York City
Weekly Letter #13

My dear Mr. Fox:

The production situation for this week was as follows:

William Farnum: Gordon Edwards did not photograph this week. He was making his preparations for beginning work on the story *The Scuttlers*. He left yesterday for San Francisco. His company, including Mr. Farnum will leave for San Francisco next Monday, and photographing will commence on Wednesday.

Mr. Farnum has not been in the best of health the last month. At the end of *The Joyous Troublemaker* he had a nervous breakdown, from which however he recovered very quickly. As a result of this condition, Mr. Farnum expressed a desire not to go away on location to make *Drag Harlan*, which, of course, was very acceptable to both Mr. Edwards and myself, as it will mean saving thousands of dollars.

Tom Mix: Flynn began photographing on *The Untamed* on Wednesday, and has been working straight thru.

During the time that Mix is working on *The Untamed*, I will work on *3 Gold Coins* and will submit to you in about ten days a list of changes and additional material to be photographed, for your approval, so that we will be able to make the changes in *3 Gold Coins* immediately after Mix finishes *The Untamed*.

William Russell: Scott Dunlap began photographing on *Twins of Suffering Creek* on Wednesday, and has been working steadily all week.

Shirley Mason: Very little work as done on the Mason picture, *The Little Wanderer* this week. Miss Mason was confined to her bed for five days with a severe attack of ptomaine poisoning, and inasmuch as she is in practically all the sequences, we were able to accomplish very little. At this writing her health is greatly improved, and she will be able to resume work on the picture Monday. We will do our best to make up for lost time.

Buck Jones: I am now preparing changes on the picture, *The Square Shooter*, and I will submit to you within a week a list of these changes for your approval, so that we can begin making this picture immediately after Buck Jones is thru with *Firebrand Trevision*.

Eileen Percy: Photographing on *Her Honor the Mayor* was finished today. This picture will be cut and shipped next week. Paul Cazeneuve, who directed this picture, has been returned to the scenario department where he will continue to edit scenarios and co-operate with me in productions.

Vivian Rich: The picture, *A World of Folly* was finished today and I have disbanded this entire company. I will have a talk with Miss Rich next week and try to get her to cancel her contract. If she is unwilling to do this, we will cast her in other parts until the end of her contract, which is August 15th.

Comedies: The production situation of the comedies this week was as follows:

We have in the cutting room the Cline (Edward) #5 picture, *Singer Midgets Scandal*; Blystone #8 picture, *His Wife's Caller*: and the Roy Del-Ruth #7 picture known as the "Country Story."

We have in the course of production the Blystone #10 picture with Clyde Cook; and Roy DelRuth #8 picture, known as the *Cop Story*. There are still being photographed additional scenes for the Cline #6 picture, *Mary's Little Lobster*, and additional scenes are also being made for the Roy DelRuth #7 picture known as the "country story".

With reference to the *Special Comedy*, in accordance with your telephone conversation with Mr. DelRuth and myself,* DelRuth understands that this picture is to be in New York by May 25th. In accordance with your instructions, when this picture is being shipped to New York, I will put a special messenger on the train with this picture, so that it will be personally delivered to you and there will be no reason for any delay in the picture reaching you, as I fully realize the importance of this picture being in New York on May 25th.

With reference to the Shirley Mason picture, *His Harvest*: I have always been of the firm opinion, and I believe I have stated this opinion to you in my previous letters, that the Shirley Mason stories should have very simple plots, due to the fact that her personality is so different than any other star's we have. In making this statement I do so in view of the pictures that I have seen with Mary Pickford and Marguerite Clark, whose type of pictures we are trying to follow with Miss Mason.

In selecting stories for Miss Mason, I have based my opinion on the fact that the audience would not want to see Miss Mason in intricate dramatic stories, but rather in simple, pleasing, wholesome stories that would be of interest both to the child and adult. It is my belief that the success of Mary Pickford and Marguerite Clark (when Miss Clark was at her top notch) was due to such stories.

However, in view of the paragraph contained in your letter, I made changes in the scenario of *The Little Wanderer* so that it would contain intrigue and complication.

General Comment: In view of a notice I have received from Mr. Leo that the motor generator sets will be on their way to Los Angeles, we have had to make some changes to lengthen and increase the capacity of our present generator building, and I have, therefore, let out a contract to make these changes with a Los Angeles concern, which will cost approximately $1500. I am enclosing herewith copy of said contract for your files. It is our endeavor to have all this work completed so that when the generators arrive in Los Angeles we can immediately begin installing them so that there will be no letup of work.

I wish to acknowledge your letter of April 20th with reference to Mr. & Mrs. Raymond Nolan. Mr. Nolan and his wife called on me today in

The first telephone communication across country between Wurtzel and Fox.

accordance with your letter, I have assigned Mr. Nolan to work as assistant cameraman at a salary of $30 a week; and Mrs. Nolan to do clerical work in our Auditing Department at a salary of $12. I will keep a very careful watch over Mr. Nolan the work he does, and when his work and capabilities warrant it, I will see that he is advanced and promoted in his work and in salary. I will do everything that I can to be of assistance to him and his wife.

One of the important requirements in our studio at present, and which will be of great economical saving to us is our immediate need for additional lamps. During the past six months, at this time and in the future, we will probably have from nine to ten companies, working almost all the time. Our present lighting equipment is insufficient to keep the companies who are working inside the studios constantly and adequately equipped.

At this writing, we have been compelled to rent fifteen lamps from outside companies to help us out. Our lighting equipment at present is as follows: 20 Small Winfield Broadsides, 65 Bach Broadsides, 55 Bach double over-heads, 50 Bach single over heads, 10 Cooper Hewitt banks, 28 Small Cooper Hewitt U tubes lamps.

The 20 small Winfield Broadsides have been in continual service, mostly on location for the past four years, and will soon be unfit for further use.

In addition to the above equipment, we have just received three Sunlight Arc lamps which were ordered thru the New York office and for which we are greatly indebted to you. They will be of great benefit and help to us.

Altho we have at present working on the stage only four dramatic companies and three comedy companies, in order to keep all of them working, we have been compelled to juggle our lamps to and fro at a great inconvenience to the companies and at a great loss of time. We have many times been compelled to ask the cameramen to get along with less lamps than they require, on account of this shortage. I therefore, kindly ask you have sent to us as soon as possible 25 Bach over heads and 25 Bach Broadside lamps. This will be of material help and aid to us, and will be greatly appreciated.

I wish to thank you very much for the very kind expression you made to me over the telephone on Tuesday, April 27th. I can assure you that the sound of your voice was a great inspiration, and made me feel as if I was right close up to you.

Everything at the studio is in excellent shape with reference to productions, and I am very pleased to be able to state that of late I have not encountered many outbursts of temperament on the part of stars and directors, and everything is going along nicely.

With kindest regards, I am

Yours very truly,
SMW.AS

New York City
May 14, 1920

Mr. S.M. Wurtzel
Los Angeles
Reply to Letter #13

My dear Sol:

William Farnum: I note what you say about Farnum. I suppose the length of time for his rest will be decided upon later.

In view of the fact that his salary materially increases for the next season, and that we would want a variety of stories on hand before he begins so that we may take our choice as we go along, it is necessary that additional material be selected for him immediately so that when he returns from his vacation, we have at least three or four set stories to select from as to which one to start with. This becomes necessary for two reasons; first, — when he returns from his vacation, Edwards will no longer direct him, (I am assuming this from past correspondence) and you will require another director for him. You can rest assured you will never be able to make the number of pictures we made with Farnum unless we have at least two first class directors with him all the time. One preparing the story, photographing and cutting, and while this is going on, another director preparing his story so that while one director is cutting and preparing his next story, the other is ready to direct him. It will take two such directors to complete the number of pictures that J. Gordon Edwards completed in any one year.

I do not believe that any other director that you engage will make more than 4 or 5 pictures during that period. Therefore it will take two directors to give me 8 pictures a year, which we require. Of course you must know that Farnum is not anxious to make 8 pictures a year. He would rather only make 4. It was only with Edwards' bull dog insistency and systematic operations that you were able to get him to give us the number of pictures we had in the past.

Of course, all this is for your personal perusal as well as the rest that I will write here.

Comedy Situation: Our letters have crossed with reference to the Comedy Situation. You already know by this time that Del Ruth is coming on for the convention and is bringing the comedy with him.

Shirley Mason: I read your paragraph with reference to Miss Mason and of the type and kind of story required with her. Also noted your reference

to Mary Pickford and Marguerite Clark. In the first place the public are
tired of the sweet pamby amby story with no sense in it. If Miss Clark
did not depend upon her extraordinary cute qualities and had real merit,
and if her stories had suspense, drama and action, her popularity would
have been increased instead of being on the down-slide.

Miss Pickford's popularity is one that no one can understand. Up to
the present she has had no competitor. We have no right to compare Miss
Mason with her, for there is no comparison so as Miss Pickford goes. We
are dealing now with Shirley Mason, and if we want to put her over with
a band and be sure that her popularity grows and that we create a big
demand for her pictures you will want her personality plus suspense,
action, drama, pathos and comedy; and all other elements that go to
make up a real interesting entertaining picture.

I do not want pictures that will depend upon her personality, but
pictures with real stories plus her personality.

I hope that this will clarify the matter and that there will be no
necessity for our corresponding on this point any further.

In addition to the above, I am going to continue a little further, on
this subject. The real big successes of the past year where only such plays
as were popularized, without a shadow of a doubt, by the popularity of
the book, or of the play. For instance, *Daddy Long Legs*: millions of copies
sold and the play ran for many successful years; *Pollyanna*: millions of
copies sold and a play that ran also for years. *Rebecca Of Sunnybrook
Farm*: millions of copies sold and a play that has been successful for years.

I have seen these three plays on the stage and have seen the motion picture versions. Neither one of them has what you would call suspense, intrigue
or dramatic action, and still they were the greatest motion pictures that Miss
Pickford every appeared in. However it was not because of her presence in
these pictures, but rather due to the wonderful recognition these three stories
received all over the world as being three of the greatest pieces of fiction written in modern times. It was this, plus Miss Pickford playing the part, though
it has no suspense or drama, that made these pictures successes.

Do not try to make that type of story with Miss Mason from an original story or from an unknown author. For a play that has a little dramatic
quality as the three above mentioned, produced from an novel that is
unknown or from an original scenario, would be valueless, not only to
Miss Mason but to Miss Pickford, or any other woman who appeared in it.

Any time that Fox Film Corporation will buy vehicles for Miss Mason
that are as popular among the American public as the above three plays, you
will rest assured that I will not ask you to re-arrange their plots, or to inject
some so-called 'heavy', or melodrama, suspense or action, but will rather
insist that the story be made as described, by the author himself or herself.

So that there will be no misunderstanding, let me say that if *Daddy Long Legs*, *Pollyanna* or *Rebecca of Sunnybrook Farm*, bore any other name and if they were never published in book form or played on the stage, they would have been ranked motion picture failures.

I trust that I have made myself clear on the subject and that you thoroughly know what I hope to accomplish with Miss Mason's pictures.

I have noted the rest of your letter carefully.

Yours very truly,

(signed) William Fox

Because of a gap in the correspondence for the last half of 1920, there remains no first hand account of the Locklear catastrophe or Fox's reaction to it. Wurtzel had finally persuaded his boss to allow him to make a picture with the daredevil aviator and Jules Furthman had prepared the script. The final stunt scenes were being filmed on the night of August 3 at the Amalgamated Oil Field at Third Street and Fairfax Avenue in Los Angeles.

For the desired effect, Locklear and his co-pilot, Milton Elliot, flew their Curtis Jenny to a height of 3,000 feet. Locklear lit a number of torches that were fastened to the plane to make it appear on fire. The craft was then allowed to glide down to an altitude of 2,000 and was put into a head spin.

Powerful searchlights were focused on the spectacle; four cameramen were furiously grinding away and it wasn't until the plane took a straight vertical dive into the ground and burst into even fiercer flames that they realized a stunt had become a horrible accident.

Later, after the burnt bodies had been dragged from the wreckage, an unsealed envelope addressed to his estranged wife was found intact in the inside pocket of Locklear's leather jacket. Inside the envelope was a blank piece of paper.

Hollywood and the Fox Film Corporation staged a heroes' funeral for the two men. A flotilla, twelve planes, and the Goodyear dirigible escorted the bodies to the train depot, while twenty mounted cowboys formed the cortege.

The Skywayman was edited and released to the Fox exhibitors in September with a hastily planned advertising campaign suggesting that it "was just as well not to mention too bluntly the death of the star while making the picture as some of the public will feel resentment towards the producers." To counteract this possibility, the company advertised that ten per cent of the profits made on the picture during its United States runs would be given to the families of the two flyers.

Ironically, the reviewers for the most part felt that the air stunts were slightly disappointing.

Convinced that Wurtzel's extravagances were either deliberate or due to a nervous breakdown, Fox sent his brother-in-law, Jack Leo, to Hollywood in February to get things back in shape.

Leo stayed on the coast for three months and although Wurtzel never missed a day away from the studio, Fox chose to filter all directives through Leo who soon realized that working conditions and price scales were vastly different in the two cities. The two men established a lasting friendship and from then on Wurtzel had a firm ally in the New York office.

Wurtzel needed his freshly restored confidence to bear up under Fox's newest outburst of wrath that descended like a cataclysm. Naively, he had produced a modernized version of "Oliver Twist" under the tile of Oliver Twist Jr. *Fox was justly horrified that his company should be releasing a picture with a character like Fagin just at the time when Henry Ford was waging an anti-Semitic campaign through the pages of the* Dearborn Independent. *He was determined to stop these attacks against his people and had threatened Ford that he would have the bi-weekly Fox newsreels show the results of every accident involving a Ford car.*

Wurtzel got around this gaffe by re-writing Dickens.

New York City
January 19, 1921

Mr. S.M. Wurtzel
Los Angeles

Reply to Weekly Letter #48

My dear Sol,

Tom Mix: I note your comment with reference to Mix.

Buck Jones: I reviewed *The Big Punch*. It is a good Buck Jones picture. However there is a much difference in value between this picture and *Just Pals* as there is between cream cheese and the full moon. *Just Pals* was one of the most artistically done pictures that I have reviewed in years. *The Big Punch* is just one more motion picture with the fact that it has less "big punch" than *Fighting Blood* had. There is no comparison between this picture and *Fighting Blood* which was the finest picture made with Farnum in two years. Changing the story simply meant losing the "big punch".

However, it is still a good Buck Jones picture, first because he gave a fine interpretation which I am sure was due to the director's ability, for his interpretation of the part in *Two Moons* was the most awful thing — for which LeSaint was responsible.

Ford (John) has proven that if Jones is properly directed he can play any part. He is daring and thrilling; has as charming personality and charming smile; strong face and therefore can play any part assigned to him providing he is properly directed.

Queen of Sheba: Of course you can readily imagine my disappointment, after this great fortune being spent on this picture, that you did not write me your opinion of this picture. Writing now of course will be of no value for by the time you receive this letter I shall have reviewed it myself.

It was your duty to have expressed your opinion, whether it be good or bad, in view of the tremendous fortune involved. That opinion should have been in my possession long before I reviewed the picture.

General Comment: With reference to your paragraphs in which you acknowledge the necessity of reducing the costs of pictures—as you state, to enable the corporation to make them without a loss—unless pictures can be made at the costs planned, I would rather shut down and stop making pictures on the coast. I don't propose to go on as in the past.

You claim the pictures now being made will not show the reduction in costs, but that the next round of pictures will—the reason being that these pictures were started before the economies were put into effect, should have materially reduced the cost of the pictures.

I have already written to Mr. Leo with reference to the liability and to charge bills against the pictures for which they incurred and not to be charged to the present cost of the pictures. That will be the only way by which we will know the exact cost of pictures being made now as well as the next round and each succeeding round. I want you to stop fooling me and I want you to stop fooling yourself and charge bills against the productions to which they properly belong.

After reading the last two pages of your letter describing the costs of sets, costs of pictures, costs of this and that and other predictions—Sol, I've heard that conversation so often, that I'm paying no attention to it. Action is what I want to see now—what the actual cost of pictures will be when completed. That's the only thing that interests me now.

I am not interested in generalities. By now you understand the great necessity of economizing as described in my communications and anxiously awaiting to see that these pictures are completed for the cost described in your letter.

It might be mighty interesting to you to read your comment from time to time which you made with reference to *Connecticut Yankee* and *Queen of Sheba* so far as the costs are concerned on these productions— the great saving you were putting into effect as a result of eliminating big sets, this and that, etc., etc., etc. You will never learn, unless you gather together all this correspondence that you sent me from time to time with reference to *Queen of Sheba* and *Connecticut Yankee*, read them and my replies, that you said so many things that didn't reach the final conclusion, that I am at a loss to know what faith to pin on your communications.

Yours very truly,
(signed) William Fox

New York City
February 15, 1921

COPY
Mr. Jack G. Leo
Hollywood Hotel, Hollywood.

Dear Jack:

The attached memorandum from Mr. Sheehan came after he reviewed *Black Beauty*. I concur with him that here is a keen interest being displayed in the animal material of that picture. Of course we have no right to use the story of "Black Beauty," but I agree with Mr. Sheehan that if we can put it into a Tom Mix picture, either at the beginning of the subject or in the middle of it — say a complete reel of horse material, it will enhance the Mix picture.

Yours sincerely
William Fox

February 14, 1921

Copy: Inter-office Memo.

Mr. William Fox:

I understand from various sources that the Vitagraph picture *Black Beauty* was quite a hit through the country and is being booked as a special attraction.

I think that the animal stuff in this picture warrants a letter being addressed to Los Angeles Studio to try and make a novelty reel of horse action in connection with a Mix picture. It would be a very unique part of a western story.

W.R. Sheehan

February 21, 1921

Copy: Inter-office Memo.

Mr. William Fox

I have reviewed all recent pictures made by the Sunshine Comedy plant in Los Angeles, and have also analyzed the comedies that are being made by other concerns and individuals. I feel that the Sunshine staff and their idea appears to be concentrated on violent and rough comedies. By this I mean that the story, gags and sequences carry with them acts of violence of a character that is bitterly opposed by censor boards and people interested in combating censorship influence and expansion.

The use of bombs, bottles labeled poison, gun play, pick-pocketing, robbery, theft, appear too frequently in Sunshine Comedies. Also the dress of our comedies is too grotesque and inhuman.

In almost every Sunshine Comedy of late there has not been a central idea or plot in connection with the picture. It is simply a series of hokum, rough gags, even depicting criminal acts, which do not get a laugh and are only interesting because of the rapid action involved.

We have discussed bathing girls and the fact the public no longer wants to see this class of picture in motion picture theatres. I understand the Coast Studio has discontinued making bathing girl pictures.

Sunshine Comedies has depended upon rapid action more than situation, story or plot for their appeal. I believe the public is tired of this type of comedy. For instance in Harold Lloyd, Buster Keaton and even in the Charlie Chaplin picture *The Kid*, there is a central idea behind each comedy and the action is much slower than Sunshine but the laughs are more frequent, wholesome and sure.

I therefore recommend that we have more plot, story and slower action, with the additional rearrangement of more modern clothes and elimination of grotesque facial make-up on the part of our actors in future Sunshine Comedies. I do not mean to kill the finish of the story by slow action, because I realize the importance of a fast finish to any comedy.

I realize that this is a vital and drastic change in the class of Sunshine Comedies, but I believe the time has arrived when the public demand the exhibitors are loud in their requests for a rearrangement in the type and style of Sunshine Comedies.

The motion picture patrons also welcome youthful characters, especially the hero and the heroine in up-to-date dress. Our characters in the love appeal in connection with comedies have been lacking personality, good looks and clean dress. Juvenile love-making in connection with comedies is always welcome.

This letter is written after months of careful analysis and study of the situation, and I recommend that the Los Angeles Studio be notified of the necessary changes to meet the conditions of the market and the public.

We have had many complaints on the photography in Sunshine Comedies. The camera work seems to be slipshod.

W.R. Sheehan

Los Angeles
March 4, 1921

COPY
Mr. Sol M. Wurtzel

I am attaching hereto copy of letter this day received from Mr. Fox for your information.

Will you be good enough and have carried out the instructions contained therein with reference to calling together directors, scenario staff, etc. so that you may convey to them imperatively that the "Fourteen Don'ts" must be lived up to.

With reference to the last paragraph, I will suggest to Mr. Fox the name of Jack Gilbert* on whom he can decide after seeing the picture *Clung*. However, if you have any other candidates in mind you may suggest them so that Mr. Fox can give you a decision on them.

Will you be good enough and see that the particular paragraph referring to Goodwin is carried out.

(Signed) Jack G. Leo
Vice President

New York City
February 26, 1921

COPY
Mr. Jack G. Leo
Hollywood Hotel, Hollywood

Dear Jack:

I just reviewed the Shirley Mason picture, *The Lamplighter*. We have no way of determining here the actual cost, but if it is within the cost you stated for these pictures, it is an achievement we hoped for.

I liked the picture very much, all except the last reel, in which the director was trying his best to finish the story and did not seem to know how. For the early part of the picture the story could have been beautifully developed where the Captain's wife could in some say refer to the person to whom the baby belonged, and then the last reel, would have been unnecessary. Most likely the last reel with the boat, etc., was probably the most expensive part of the picture and the most uninteresting.

I also reviewed *Oliver Twist Jr*. This story is based on Dickens's "Oliver Twist" and therefore should not have been made. The original picture† was made by Jimmy Young with Marie Doro, who looked the little bit of a thing. In our *Oliver Twist* we use a long, lean, lanky six foot boy,‡ who looks more like a senior than a junior, as a result of his height. This is not the only defect of the picture.

---

*John Gilbert — young actor, later the popular screen lover. †Released by Lasky-Universal in 1916. ‡Harold Goodwin — who played a 17-year-old Oliver in this contemporary version.

During these days of Ford's propaganda against the Jews, it is hardly befitting that this Company should attempt to make or revive the hatred that Dickens's caused when he originally wrote "Oliver Twist," in characterizing Fagan as a Jew.

To make it possible for release I have had 75 scenes in which Fagan appears taken out for two reasons:

First: That no censorship board in America today is willing to pass any picture in which there appears a character, whether he be Jew or Christian, whose profession is to teach boys to steal, or where his profession is to be a fence for stolen goods.

While on this point, I am herewith attaching a story that appeared in the New York World, and most likely in other newspapers throughout the country, issued by Jesse L. Lasky, called "Lasky's Fourteen Points of Don'ts" in connection with pictures. Mr. Lasky violated a confidence of the meeting of Manufacturers* in issuing this statement to the press, which he had proposed by motion at the last two meetings of the National Association, and each time his motion was lost. The consensus of opinion being that all manufacturers in the future should devote their time and energy in making clean, wholesome pictures, the type and kind that will necessitate no censorship boards. It was unanimously agreed that to give the article to the press was confession that the Lasky Company had made pictures that were vile and indecent, and now resolved by these points not to do it again. If this article was sent out by all the manufacturers, then it would be a confession that they all did these things.

This, however, does not change the consensus of opinion of all manufacturers who belong to the National Association, that future pictures must contain these "Dont's" that now appear in the attached article.

It is important and imperative that you call together your directorial forces and scenario writers, and read this to them, and tell them that Fox Film Corporation does not want to make any pictures to which there could be the slightest objection by the population of this country, and if any director should insist upon making vile and indecent scenes, or scenario writers should conceive that which we call "don't" today, we have no further use for them. We want no one around who cannot conceive and direct things that will meet with the approval of the censorship boards.

Second: The second reason for not wanting to make "Oliver Twist" at this time is because of Ford's attitude, and to picture Fagan as a Jew encourages race hatred.

Sheehan and I have had a conference with reference to Goodwin and we have reached the conclusion that after he has completed the present picture

*National Association of the Motion Picture Industry.

he is not to be starred in any more. If his contract is for a further length of time, then he is to be used to play parts in pictures but not to be starred. If this is not satisfactory to the gentleman, you are authorized to abrogate the present contract.

This leaves us in an awkward position, for we have only on the 20th Century program Buck Jones and Eileen Percy. Therefore, if you any spare time, inquire as to who is available and whether if engaged, he or she will be a real asset to the 20th Century brand. Don't pledge yourself or engage anyone. We likewise are making a search here, and before we reach a decision, it would have to be the result of much discussion, and after we have absolutely decided that the person selected would be an asset.

It is a pity that the boy won't do, because as things are now, the public are more interested in pictures in which men appear than those in which girls appear. Therefore, if there is a likely candidate at Los Angeles, I would prefer a male to a female. At this particular time the pictures that are most in demand are those with men. For illustration: Thomas Meighan, Wallace Reed, Tom Mix and Charles Ray, and you will find that no woman in the business compares with their drawing power. Whether there is available a young man who has made a real hit in one, two, or three pictures, and has a right to be considered as a candidate, you should know because you are in the film market.

Yours sincerely,
William Fox

New York City
March 24th, 1921

Mr. S.M. Wurtzel
Los Angeles

My dear Sol:

You no doubt by this time are acquainted with the fact that every print of *Oliver Twist Jr.* shipped to every exchange throughout the United States, has been returned to New York.

This has been brought about by the tremendous volume of protests coming from every corner of the country, voicing vehemently the protests of every intellectual Hebrew throughout the country.

A picture of the type and kind referred to herein above might not have brought the storm of protest, were it made under the supervision of a producer who was a non-Jew. You have heaped upon my shoulders an embarrassment that is inexplicable, by allowing a director to take a distinctly Jewish type and portray him as Fagin. There is no excuse for your having permitted this, as there were other liberties taken with this story, and therefore, the brunt of responsibility cannot be shifted to Charles Dickens.

There is not doubt in my mind, that while Dickens was a great writer, his trend of thought and his feeling was evidenced in many of his works against the Jew. But how, I should like to know, how in the world, you as a Hebrew, could permit depicting one of your own kind as has been done in the picture *Oliver Twist Jr.* It was just as simple to make it one of any other race, but it seems as though you have lost the obligation to your race and kind. You have permitted an insipid, narrow-minded, bigoted director to undo in a single picture all that I have striven to build up in the past ten years.

An irreparable injury has been done both to myself and to the corporation at a time when anti-Semitism is rampant throughout the country; at a time when it behooves every man, woman, and child who has the blood of a Jew running through their veins, to stand firmly together; at a time when a deed of this type is added fuel for those whom we must combat; and furthermore, at a time when all the words in the world would be insufficient try and extinguish a flame that only needs fuel of this type to fan it into a raging conflagration.

To believe that a picture of this type was produced under the auspices of a Jew, is unbelievable and unthinkable. You are ordered imperatively, that in the future you desist from this type of characterization. You are not to permit any director to include or make part of his story, the Jew, vilified in any manner, shape or form.

I look forward to an immediate acknowledgment of this letter, setting forth what is required of you in the future, with reference to the subject matter contained here-in-above.

Very truly yours,
(signed) William Fox

P.S. I am attaching hereto just a few of the letters that have received by me, showing you the various sections of the country where complaints are emanating from. After reading these letters, will you be good enough and return same for my files.

Los Angeles
March 30, 1921

Mr. William Fox
New York City

My dear Mr. Fox:

I wish to acknowledge your letter of March 24th, and deeply regret the occurrence of the picture *Oliver Twist Jr.*

When I originally discussed the making of this picture with Mr. Sheehan who was here at the time, I never had any idea in my mind that Jewish Societies were antagonistic to Charles Dickens's *Oliver Twist*. Had I had any inkling of this fact, you may be sure I never would have permitted this story to have been made.

It seems to me, however, that this picture need not be a total loss because by making a limited number of new scenes in which we could portray another character of a different type for the character of Grimes or Fagan in the story. It would give the picture an entirely new aspect, and the main title of the picture could be changed. I am offering this as a suggestion as you stated in your letter you had all prints returned to the Home Office.

I have never, at any time in the making of pictures, permitted the character of the Jew to be portrayed or caricaturized, with the exception of this story, which to my mind had always been considered as one of the classics and a book that is read in the public schools and every school. The knowledge that I have just learned, that this book is objected to by Jewish Societies was a complete surprise to me; and indeed regret this occurrence for I feel as keenly as you the embarrassment that the release of this picture has caused you.

I note your instructions that no Jewish characters are to be portrayed in any pictures of any kind, nature or description, which instructions I can assure you will be absolutely followed out.

I am returning herewith the enclosures you sent me in your letter of March 24th.

Yours very truly,
SMW.AS

New York City
June 3, 1921

Mr. Sol M. Wurtzel
Los Angeles

My dear Sol:
I have read Mr. Leo's letter to you dated June 2nd. I consider the terms and language he employs rather mild, in view of the present circumstances. Mr. Leo tried to convey to you that exhibition throughout the country is in a chaotic condition and that our purpose in keeping down the cost of film is to help the exhibitor. That is incorrect. The exhibitor is asking us for no help. He has too many companies to choose from and does not require the help of Fox Film Corporation.

We will be unable to sell him our pictures this coming season for the prices we will be obliged to quote in accordance with the cost as it is now mounting in Los Angeles. We will be outside of his reach, and therefore we will find that the gross revenue of Fox Film Corporation will be materially effected and it will compel us to entirely shut down and discontinue the making of film. The exhibitors will continue to operate whether Fox Film Corporation makes pictures or not. It is Fox Film Corporation that will have to cease and not the theatres.

All those who have been with Fox Film Corporation from its inception have given not only their energy, labor and best efforts, but have given part of their very lives to the success of this company, and it is unfair to these men to do anything that will tend to destroy that which they all labored for so hard to build up.

The condition as stated in Mr. Leo's letter, with reference to the amount of negative exposed for the various pictures he names, to my way of thinking, is an outrage — and that is putting it mildly. It is conclusive proof that your system of control is lax, and that the directors are making these pictures on a catch-as-catch-can basis, and not on a systematic basis.

If they are directors of the type and kind that do not know what they are doing prior to the making of the story, we are better off to dismiss the directorial staff, and get a new set of men. The making of pictures is no longer a mystery. It is now on a sound basis as a result of a great deal of costly experience, and there is no excuse for any man over-exposing the number of feet of negative as disclosed by Mr. Leo's communication to you.

Mr. Leo lays great stress on the value of exposed negative and positive in connection with the making of pictures, and shows the value, in money, that has been wasted for over-exposed negative and positive. This would not have happened had the proper number of feet been exposed, instead of shooting wildly and promiscuously. The real cost is the waste of time of the directors, his staff, and performers who are taking part in the pictures made.

This communication is sent to you not as a request to change conditions, but as a demand to change them, and to change them immediately, otherwise it will be necessary for Mr. Leo or myself to go to Los Angeles, so that we may prevent this disastrous destruction of Fox Film Corporation.

Yours very truly,
(signed) William Fox

Los Angeles
September 27, 1921

(Copy)
Mr. William Fox
New York City

My dear Mr. Fox:

I wish to acknowledge receipt of your letter of September 21st, and I have carefully noted contents containing therein. I particularly noted the paragraphs with reference to your disappointment with the Buck Jones picture, *Riding with Death* which was directed by Jaccard, and the Jack Gilbert picture, *Hidden Spring* directed by Dillon (Jack).

With reference to the picture, *Riding with Death*, it was my opinion after I reviewed the picture that it was a good Buck Jones picture and made at a reasonable cost; and for that reason I permitted Jaccard to continue.

With reference to the Gilbert picture, *The Hidden Spring*, I of course agree with you that it is not to be compared with *Gleam O'Dawn*; however, I do not consider it a bad picture. This story was purchased at the same time we purchased the book *Gleam O'Dawn*; and at the time we purchased it; we did not realize that we had to play Gilbert in a certain type of character.

With reference to Furthman (Jules) writing the story *The Hidden Spring*, this is incorrect. Furthman wrote the scenario of the story and the book was written by Clarence B. Kelland which was purchased for us thru the New York scenario department. My understanding, however, was that Kelland's name could not be used in connection with the story.

I have realized in the past few months, in view of the large quantity of production that is going on at Los Angeles Studios—we have at present 10 dramatic and 5 comedy companies—that we must institute a radical change in production policy. At the present time the making of the comedies is organized into a department which is being supervised Mr. Seiler, and to which I also devote a great deal of time. In the making of feature pictures I have practically no help at all. I do not believe that one man can have the supervision of 10 feature companies and get maximum results. It is only natural that some pictures just receive more attention than others.

I will be frank to state that I believe the quality of all the pictures can be a great deal improved and likewise a great deal of time can be saved in the photographing of the pictures, in getting proper and quicker preparation of stories, if the making of the feature pictures was subdivided so that we have one man taking care of five companies and another man taking care of five companies.

About a year ago I made this suggestion to you, and that was that if you had a man in New York who you could send out here to supervise four or five companies and I could supervise the remainder, it is my belief that the quality of the pictures could be a great deal improved and the cost minimized. I think this matter is one of greatest importance.

It is my belief if I could have four hours personal conversation with you on the matter we could accomplish more in that time that we could by all the correspondence in the world. I, therefore, suggest that I go to New

York to see you, if only for one day. The entire trip would take ten days from the time I leave Los Angeles until the day I get back, so that I could take up with you in person production matters. Will you, therefore, be good enough on receipt of this letter to telegraph me if this meets with your approval. Although we are at the height of production at this time, our productions now are in such form that this would be a very feasible time to do it.

Yours very truly,
SMW.as

Although Wurtzel did not get Fox's permission to go to New York in October, he did make it in December for one week. For the first time in four and half years he conferred with his boss in person, and was able to observe the accomplishments of the East coast establishment for himself.

The following letter sums up all that had been discussed by the two men and agreed to by Wurtzel. The final letter is addressed to J. Gordon Edwards who was making several Biblical pictures for Fox, in Europe. From its tone Wurtzel showed that he had his human side too, even a sense of humor.

New York City
December 16, 1921

Mr. William Fox

Dear Mr. Fox:

In accordance with our conversation this afternoon, I am giving you herewith my summary of the various talks we have had during my visit here, and my understanding of what is expected of the West Coast Studios when I return there, and what we will accomplish.

The situation with reference to the future companies is as follows:

Tom Mix :Tom Mix is now completing the picture which is being directed by Lynn Reynolds. Reynolds will continue to direct Tom Mix. We have also arranged to engage as an alternating director for Mix, Arthur Rosson. When I return to California I will meet with Rosson, and will arrange the salary. Rosson now is working with Mix on a story of romantic love interest. Every possible effort will be made on this picture to cater to the women and girls of the audience, and we will have Mix dressed up wherever possible, this being in line to make Mix pictures attractive to feminine audiences as well as masculine audiences, and the policy in the future will be to alternate pictures of this type with Western stories of the type of *Trail*, etc.

Our production arrangement with reference to Mix for the next year will be as in the past, on a basis of ten pictures per year, as it is only in this way that we can expect to make Mix pictures at a reasonable cost, so that as soon as one picture is finished, the alternating director, who has in the meantime been preparing the story, will immediately start with Mix, so that we will not have Mix and the staff, waiting around between pictures and pile up a large cost before he started photographing on the pictures.

I am sure that the past cordial relationship that has existed between Mix and the management is going to continue, because I realize the importance of Mix being kept in a happy frame of mind, and that he must be kept contented, as this is the best way we can get what we wish to attain from him.

Mix pictures will average between 4200 and 4400 feet in length. As I understand it from Mr. Sheehan, preferably 4200 feet, this to include titles. This we have faithfully followed in the past year, the average length of the Mix pictures being 4200 feet.

Dustin Farnum: Under no circumstances will any picture with Dustin Farnum be over 4500 feet in length, not only when his picture is cut and finished, but when the scenario is prepared we will see that only enough scenes are in it, so that the scenario when photographed will not be more than 4500 of compact, dramatic action with titles. No long-drawn-out sequences, no walks or exits, but get to the point, and we will immediately to the next one.

In viewing the pictures which were directed here by Dawley (J. Searles) and Carewe (Edwin), I paid particular attention to this point. To my mind on of the best examines of this method was pursued in the picture *Glean O'Dawn*, which did not contain a single walk or exit, and every scene meant something to the picture. In this way we were able to have an intense, interesting, dramatic story in 4500 feet. In the construction of these dramatic stories comedy relief will be inserted in a logical manner to relieve dramatic situations.

We have already selected the next two stories for Dustin Farnum: *When Iron Turns to Gold* and *West*. The picture *When Iron Turns to Gold*, director Durning,* who has been directing Farnum in the past and who will continue to direct him, will begin photographing after the first of the year. Sets for this picture are now being erected.

I have already had many talks with Durning with reference to the length of the Farnum pictures and the costs, and we have arranged our schedule for the making of these pictures so that they will be photographed each within four weeks, without having to work nights or Sundays and having to pay extra money for overtime. I have made it clear to Durning that his future with the Company depends upon his completing these pictures under these conditions.

*Married to Shirley Mason.

Buck Jones: As soon as Buck Jones returns to Los Angeles which will be on December 27th, Durning will immediately make the additional scenes for *Fast Mail*, on which he has two days work with Jones, and then we have some odd scenes that he can make with Jones on Sunday, as he appears in them. This will complete the picture.

One of the first things I will do when I get back will be to locate two corking good directors who can make pictures of the Buck Jones type, who have an understanding of the human heart interest and drama which will be inserted in future Buck Jones' pictures. Although we will retain the stunts as we have in the past, more attention and thought will be given to making the stories human, as in *Just Pals*. Every effort will be made to insert sequence in the stories, so as to give Buck an opportunity to dress up. I realize the great importance attached to future Buck Jones pictures, so that Buck will be built up and so that he will progress.

Shirley Mason: In accordance with my conversation with you this afternoon, pictures of the type of *Little Mother* and *The Lamplighter* are the type of pictures that exhibitors want with Shirley Mason and her future stories will be selected along these lines. I believe, however, that it would be a good thing to give Miss Mason roles where she can dress up and wear good clothes, as this always lends distinction to a picture, and is of interest to women and girls.

I will devote every possible effort and energy to the Shirley Mason pictures, as I realize she is the only woman we have in the Fox Film Corporation list of feature players, and her production, as I told Mr. Leo, have been arranged so they will be photographed in approximately three and a half weeks, so that the cost of the pictures without Miss Mason's salary will be from $18,00 to $20,000. This I am sure we can accomplish, because Miss Mason is paid by the picture.

Jack Gilbert: I have already selected Jack Gilbert's story. The title is "The Land of Beginning Again." This gives Gilbert a picturesque role. The story is laid in the Foreign Legion of Algeria. This in itself is a picturesque background, and Gilbert has a very fine and dramatic part to portray. Future stories with Gilbert will be laid along the lines and type *Gleam O'Dawn*, where Gilbert will have a romantic, picturesque character to portray. I do not think we can make these pictures for less than $25,000.

Emmett Flynn: I have a complete understanding of what you want of Emmett Flynn in *A Fool There Was*. The changes to be made in the story, using indifference instead of lust and passion, making it a human interest story, building up the man to a big height of power and influence, and making him a wonderful husband and father, so that when he does fall, his fall will be a direct contrast, and a tremendous lesson will be taught by the story.

Before the cast is engaged I will wire you the names so that you can approve of them. I have fully in mind all your wishes in regard to this production, its sets, salaries to be paid to actors, and that not a single actor or actress will be engaged unless they are personally engaged by Mr. Bird* through me. I will decide on the salaries to be paid.

I have in mind that the best way to obtain results is to have perfect friendship and harmony between the directors and every executive of the studio, and I am going to arrange to have Mr. Bird and Mr. Flynn get together so that they can work in a more harmonious way.

I do not anticipate the least bit of difficulty with Flynn, for I am sure that the talk you have had with Flynn, at which I was present, and in which you explained to him that any production which he makes, in order to be of benefit to the corporation, if it is not made at a cost which will enable the Corporation to make a profit, it is better not to make it. As you said to him, you were not going to set a cost for *A Fool There Was*, but that you were going to have Mr. Flynn set an example for himself in the making of this picture.

Comedies: Comedy productions will continue as heretofore, except that they will be increased with the arrival of Lupino Lane.† Mr. Leo stated his salary to me, and I am of the firm belief that in order to make Lane's pictures at a reasonable cost, we will need two directors. I realize the tremendous importance of Lane's pictures and every effort will be made to give him the best directors and the best vehicles.

Clyde Cook: Immediately upon my arrival I will get Cook's signature to the new contract. I believe that the new arrangement with him, paying him by the picture, and likewise of his director being paid by the pictures, will have the beneficial effect on the cost that is desired. In order for Cook to earn the money he wishes, he will have to make eight pictures a year, likewise his director, and this will automatically decrease the cost of the pictures.

Immediately upon my return to Los Angeles, I will have a conference with Mr. Bird and the other studio department heads, so we can make substantial decreases in the overhead of the studio. By consolidating various departments, and by diminishing and dismissing such employees as will be surplus by the combining of departments, and by checking very carefully every dollar that is spent for purchases, rentals, etc., and the shipping to us of the furniture from New York, will practically eliminate the rental of modern furniture, so that we will probably only have to rent rugs, pictures and hand props, which will all reduce the costs. We now have the carpentering and electrical and laboring staffs down to a minimum.

Every director will be given notice that absolutely no overtime work

Manager of the dramatic department. †Of the famous English family of acrobats.

will be permitted, and no night work will be allowed except on exterior
night scenes, and these will be eliminated in every place possible.

Directors will be given to understand that they are expected and will
photograph from nine o'clock in the morning until 4:30 or 5 o'clock in
the afternoon, and a violation of these rules will mean their job.

In the past almost all directors have been faithfully abiding by this rule.

Our system at present with reference to extras, and which is working out very well, is that wherever more than ten extras are requisitioned
by a director, it is referred to me, and then I will personally approve or
disapprove of the extra amount. I am sure you will note that in the pictures that have been sent in the past ten months, that we have greatly dis-
couraged the use of extras.

Stories: Very careful supervision will be given to stories, selected and
arranged so that we use a minimum number of principal characters, as
we can get more intense drama in a story with three or four or five characters, and the story is easier to photograph, and the plot can more easily
be told, than if we had a dozen characters. This automatically decreases
the photographing time and the salaries to be paid by extra characters,
and insures a better picture.

Our Slogan in the selection of stories will be: *Human Heart Interest,
Intense Drama with Comedy Relief.*

Regarding sets. I personally approve of every set that is erected in the
studio, both as to the size of the set, its cost, and its necessity in the picture.

Regarding the salaries to be paid to actors; I am sure that we are going
to show excellent results, for I have fully in mind that what you want in the
future, is not a $75 actor for $75, but a $200 or $250 for this amount, and I
am going to personally supervise this end of it, together with Mr. Bird.

No actor or actress will be engaged by any director. Directors will
be asked to offer suggestion as to whom they would like, and if they
are satisfactory, and the salaries can be satisfactorily arranged, we will
engage the, for I believe the director who handles the actor, some def-
erence should be given to his judgment as to the type and quality of
actor he requires, but only on condition that the salary is satisfactory.
Your statement in the talks that you have given me with regard to conditions of the industry have made it absolutely clear to me that
absolutely no picture shall be made unless such a picture can earn a
profit to the Corporation, and every director who is working for the
Corporation in Los Angels, and who will be engaged in the future, will
have a clear understanding of this, and that we will not engage a director
to experiment with, but we will make sure that the first picture every
director makes will be a corking good picture at a reasonable cost. Only
directors will be engaged who have made good in the past, and

who have something to show for themselves, and their pictures will be judged as fine productions from the scenes of the pantomime and the characters, and not by the titles that the characters speak.

I have accomplished more during my stay here, and have learned more, so that when I go back to Los Angeles, I go back with a complete and thorough knowledge and understanding of what is to be done in the future.

Very truly yours,

Los Angeles
January 9, 1922

Mr. J. Gordon Edwards
Excelsior Hotel
Rome, Itly.

My dear J. Gordon:

I received your card from Rome and want to thank you very much for your kind wishes for the New Year. Mrs. Wurtzel and Lillian and Paul (whom you have not yet seen) join me in extending to you and Angie our very best wishes for a bright and prosperous New Year.

You will no doubt be surprised to learn that I was in New York about a month ago and saw Mr. Fox. We had quite a lull in work here and as it was the first opportunity I have had in four and one-half years, I seized the opportunity and went to New York, and spent a wild week there. I had some very fine talks with Mr. Fox. He told me he was expecting your first picture *Nero*, and I was very sorry I did not see it before I left New York. Mr. Fox took great pride in telling me he felt sure it was going to be a wonderful picture, made at half the cost of *Queen of Sheba*. This last was said with special emphasis.

Just as I came to this point of my letter, Tom Mix walked in and he said that if you have any more chariot races or things of that kind, or if you wanted to slaughter some gladiators, he is always at your command. Tom felt he could have been of great aid to you in the burning of Rome. Tom has taken up the violin so he could have fiddled while Rome was destroyed. Tom asked me to extend to you and Mrs. Edwards his kindest regards.

Queen of Sheba opened in Los Angeles at the Philharmonic Auditorium and played six weeks. The amount of profit shown was not large, however this was not the fault of the picture. Business conditions have been terrible, and I am still convinced that the public is not yet educated to a $2.00 scale. All road companies of all big productions such as *Over the Hill, Sheba, Theodora, Way Down East, The Four Horsemen*, have been called in.

*Theodora** played at the California Theatre for two weeks. The first

---

*An Italian super-spectacle released by Goldwyn.

three days it did good business and then dropped like a log. The reason was very simple. I saw the picture. It contains big sets and thousands of people who do nothing but run around, and as far as the lions are concerned, my impression was that in Europe one could obtain the most ferocious lions because it is so near the base of supplies. But the lions in our Sunshine Comedies were more ferocious than all the lions in *Theodora*. During one of the supposedly big scenes where the lions rush into the arena, one lion calmly sits down and paws his nose. However, the big fault with *Theodora*, was that no one knew what it was all about. The story was entirely lost, which proves that your theory is correct. The big sets and crowds should be a background for the drama and story, and the story should come first all the time.

People in the trade who have seen Griffith's *Two Orphans* which he has renamed *The Orphans of the Storm* say it is Griffith's greatest picture. He has changed the story so that he has included the old fall of the Bastille and guillotine. It has just opened in New York. Some of the critics praise it highly and some don't.

When I was in New York Mr. Fox wanted me to see Millarde's picture, but it was not completed and in the rough, and he changed his mind. Millarde has beaten Griffith's records by about two months. Harry Millarde started to work on his picture the same time that Griffith stated *Two Orphans* and when I left New York Millarde was still photographing some scenes. Tom Mix says that Millarde's speed was due to the intoxicating stimulants he drinks about four o'clock on the set every afternoon — otherwise known as tea.

While in New York I reviewed a picture with Mr. Fox that was made by Serle Dawley and Edwin Carew, supervised by Julius Steger. There is still a great deal to be done on the picture although both directors have since sung their swan song with the corporation.

I think the New York studio and building is wonderful, and Mr. Fox personally took me around and showed me the place. However, I still prefer Los Angeles. I do not see how people can live in New York, take part in the night life and still make pictures. It can't be done!

Saw Bill Farnum in New York, He is looking great, however, he was sore at me because we made *Monte Cristo* without him. I did not want to tell him that he could not play the first part which called for a young man of about 20, as I wanted to spare his feelings. Farnum swears he will never look at the picture.

Here's hoping your new picture, *Shepard King* will knock 'em dead. A line from you once in a while I will greatly appreciate.

Sincerest love and regards to you and Angie and the entire family from myself and my family.

Sincerely yours,

Conclusion

Wurtzel never forgot the lessons in economy that he learned under William Fox's tutelage. After the founder was forced out of his own company and Sidney Kent eventually became president, Wurtzel was given a separate production unit on the Western Avenue lot. Back in the old studio, he surrounded himself with former Fox employees who had fallen on hard times. Men who had to leave the industry because they could not get jobs were given new opportunities. Among them, Alan Dwan and George Marshall were able to re-establish themselves as extremely successful directors with careers lasting into the sixties.

Without interference from the new regime, Wurtzel produced the "bread and butter" pictures that consistently showed a profit. While the big, prestige productions were being made in the new modern Fox Movietone City near Beverly Hills, he was turning out his low budget, money-making "B's" that kept the company from going under financially on several occasions.

In these pictures, Wurtzel developed many of the stars that later became the biggest assets of 20th Century–Fox. He made the studio's first two pictures with Shirley Temple that established her as the number one box office attraction, at which point the main studio took her for the "A" films. His production of *Bright Eyes* with Temple cost $220,000 and made a profit of $1,353,000. To provide a contrast to the cloying charm of the dimpled Shirley, he popularized the young Jane Wither — a mischievous brat with straight dark hair.

When the studio didn't know what to do with Will Rogers for the remainder of his contract, they handed him to Wurtzel who then made two hit pictures with the humorist and had him signed to a new contract. He also pioneered the "series" pictures that became to popular in the thirties: Charlie Chan, Mr. Moto, and The Jones Family.

Many years later, Philip Scheuer, the Film Editor of the *Los Angeles Times*, was to write in retrospect referring to Sol Wurtzel and his association with 20th Century–Fox, "There were occasions in which it looked suspiciously as if the tail was wagging the dog."

Appendix: Biographical Notes on Sol M. Wurtzel

Solomon Maximillian Wurtzel was born in 1890 to European immigrant parents Adolf and Pauline. He grew up running the streets on the lower east side of New York with his four brothers. Adolf was extremely strict and Pauline was revered as "My Gutsalika Mother," my sainted mother.

Four of the five brothers worked in show business. Sol was the CEO for the West Coast offices of Fox Film Studios. Harry became an agent representing such talents as John Ford, Henry King, and Gene Autry. (Once these artists became successful, they left him.) Ben headed the construction department for Fox Studios. Sam, the youngest, who got Sol his first job with Fox, was a unit manager at Fox Studios.

In 1919 Sam proposed to Sarah (aka Sid) in New York, asking her to come to the West Coast with him as he was going to work for his brother Sol. Sid agreed on the condition that she could bring her parents, siblings and their spouses. As a result approximately 50 people relocated to the West Coast to work for Sol at the studio.

Sol married Marion in 1915. They had two children: Paul, who became an assistant director, and Lillian, who compiled the manuscript for this book.

Sol left the studios in 1945 when the studio was beginning to seek other personnel to produce the B movies. He began his own production company and produced 18 feature films, which were released through Fox.

Sol M. Wurtzel retired in 1950 and died in 1958.

Index